PLAUTUS
THREE COMEDIES

MASTERS OF LATIN LITERATURE

EDITORS: FREDERICK AHL, DISKIN CLAY,
DOUGLASS PARKER, JON STALLWORTHY

This series aims to help reestablish the importance and intrinsic interest of Latin literature in an age which has rejected the Latin literary model in favor of the Greek. We plan to make available, in modern English-language versions, influential Latin works, especially poetry, from the third century B.C. to the eighteenth century of our own era. By "influential works" we mean not only those commonly read in the classroom today, either in the original or in translation, but also those which shaped literature in their own and in subsequent times, yet have now either lost or been dismissed from their places among the "Great Books" of our culture.

ALSO IN THE SERIES:

Seneca. *Three Tragedies*. Translated by Frederick Ahl.

PLAUTUS
THREE COMEDIES

Miles Gloriosus • *Pseudolus* • *Rudens*

TRANSLATED AND WITH

AN INTRODUCTION BY

PETER L. SMITH

CORNELL UNIVERSITY PRESS

ITHACA AND LONDON

First published 1991 by Cornell University Press.
First printing, Cornell Paperbacks, 1991.

Printed in the United States of America

Library of Congress Cataloging-in-Publication Data

Plautus, Titus Maccius.
    [Selections. English. 1991]
    Three comedies / Plautus ; translated and with an introduction by Peter L. Smith.
        p.   cm.   (Masters of Latin literature)
    Contents: Miles gloriosus — Pseudolus — Rudens.
    ISBN 0-8014-2355-4 (cloth : alkaline paper). — ISBN 0-8014-9594-6 (paper :
alkaline paper)
    1. Plautus, Titus Maccius—Translations, English. I. Smith, Peter L. (Peter
Lawson), 1933- . II. Title.   III. Series.
PA6570.A3S65 1991
872'.01—dc20   90-41383

Contents

General Introduction

Plautus and Roman Comedy

The earliest of Rome's surviving literary achievements, comic drama flowered during a crucial formative period in Roman history, the late third and early second centuries B.C. This was the era of Rome's swift rise to international prominence. Within living memory, the Roman state had grown from a peninsular republic to a Mediterranean superpower. It had won mastery over the ancient Greek cities of southern Italy, had acquired Sicily, had defeated mighty Carthage in the First Punic War, and by 202 B.C. (only three or four years after Plautus composed his *Miles Gloriosus*) had ended the Second Punic War against Hannibal. These remarkable events were profoundly affecting the social, economic, and cultural life of Italy.

During this period, as Rome fully encountered Greek civilization, Latin literature sprang to life. Romans were of course well aware of Greece, having coexisted for many centuries with the Greek colonies of southern Italy and Sicily; but the older civilization had seemed alien, remote, hostile. Now it was an extension of Rome, and close contact brought about a rush of interest and a thirst for Greek culture. Not even the most jingoistic Roman could fail to acknowledge the magnificence of the Greek achievement, especially in art and literature. Fortunately, there seemed to be no overpowering shock wave of national inferiority: the ancient political and spiritual traditions of Italy had sufficient strength to ward off any feelings of inadequacy. Thus, without loss of pride or self-confidence, Rome joyously embraced the established tradition of Greek literature. Less than a generation after the fall of Tarentum, poetic treasures were being borrowed from Greek epic and drama as actively as art treasures were being removed from the sanctuaries of the Greek world.

Before the literary riches could be shared, they had to be translated from

I

Greek into the "barbaric" Latin language. This was a novel challenge for the pioneer craftsmen who undertook the task of bringing Greek drama to Roman audiences. Even if they were to attempt nothing more than prosaic literal translation, they would need great skill and sensitivity. But Roman dramatists were not content with mere translation. Partly out of a need to accommodate local Italian traditions, partly out of a desire for innovation and experiment, partly out of a natural wish to play with the rich verbal resources of an unexploited language, poets such as Naevius and Plautus began to write comedies that were not so much translations as adaptations or imitations of Greek originals. The Greeks themselves had had the highest respect for creative imitation: their own dramatists offered proof of the rewards to be gained from reworking familiar thematic material. That Roman drama should continue to be based on Greek models was therefore no token of sterility or timidity, but was instead the rejuvenation of an ancient Hellenic tradition.

The models chosen by the Roman poets Naevius and Plautus, and by their famous comic successor Terence, were drawn from the period of Greek New Comedy—that is, of Attic comedy in the Hellenistic Age. Just as Athens after Alexander's conquest was a very different community from the fifth-century city-state, so had her comedy evolved a long way from Aristophanes. The poets of New Comedy—Diphilus, Philemon, and the great master Menander—had no interest in boisterous political satire; their concern was for the depiction of character, sentiment, and gently amusing romantic entanglement. Occasionally, New Comedy might still allow a tragic parody or mythological travesty, but such works were more characteristic of an earlier phase. For the most part, the Hellenistic stage was peopled with down-to-earth types, many of whom were given a memorable dramatic individuality. It was a comic society of courtesans, pimps, and lovers, of soldiers, slaves, and parasites—a cosmopolitan demimonde. Today we are poorly equipped either to enjoy or to evaluate this Greek theater: even after exciting modern papyrus finds, the extant remains of Menander are scant and may not represent his best work. In Plautus' Rome, a century after his death, and throughout antiquity, Menander's reputation was unsurpassed.

Whatever our knowledge of Menander and his contemporaries, we can establish the hybrid nature of Roman comedy, which (in the extant Latin plays) seems rarely to be direct translation. Quite apart from individual inventiveness, there was enough Italian blood in the comic pedigree to prevent any play from becoming merely a pale copy of a Greek original. Most prominent was the influence of the Atellan farce, a Roman import from Campania, itself the offshoot of a south Italian Greek farce known as *phlyax*. This robust genre featured four stock characters, similar to the types of *commedia dell'arte*: Maccus, a stupid and gluttonous clown; Dossenus, a clever hunchback; Bucco, a braggart; and Pappos, a silly old man. Although Greek New Comedy had also had its stock masks, these Italian types were obviously more broadly drawn and were acted in a tradition of stylized buffoonery. It can be seen at once that such a tradition would develop theatrical tastes that might find unappetizing the rather bland refinement of sentimental comedy. A second influence from the Italian peninsula was that of Etruscan music and dance, which had been part of Roman public entertainment for a hundred and fifty years before Plautus. It should be realized, too, that there had been a more than rudimentary tradition of native Latin poetry, employing verse forms strongly accentual in character, before Romans had any substantial exposure to Greek literature.

No Roman poet, therefore, was likely to produce a literal Latin version of Greek New Comedy, except perhaps as an academic exercise. And we must understand that early Roman comedy was never academic: this was popular entertainment, staged in Rome for a restless and impolite audience that would not hesitate, if the play was dull, to abandon the theater in favor of rival attractions. It is a measure of Plautus' success that he was able to gauge the taste of his audience, achieve enormous popularity and fame, and so educate the Roman theatrical public that the next generation would accept the less exuberant approach of Terence, whose plays were closer in spirit to Menander and Greek New Comedy.

About Plautus we have virtually no certain biographical data. His traditional dates (254–184 B.C.) are credible enough, and his birthplace (Sarsina, in the region of Umbria) is well attested. Otherwise, we have only the usual apocryphal anecdotes. The full name Titus Maccius Plautus may have been a facetious theatrical pseudonym.[1] Very likely he took the name Maccius from his experience in acting the stock role of Maccus the clown in the Atellan farce; certainly his plays show unmistakable signs of firsthand theatrical knowledge, and an acting career seems probable. Was it usual for such a man—a lowly Roman actor from northern Italy—to command the Greek language and the Greek comic repertoire? Our knowledge of Plautus' environment is too slight to provide an answer to this intriguing question.

Time has been kind to Plautus: twenty plays have survived in a more or less complete state, as compared with the one complete comedy and assorted fragments of Menander. The twenty extant comedies show a considerable variety of plot. There are plays of innocent mistaken identity, of deliberate deception (often managed by a scheming slave), of romantic or domestic complication, even one (*Amphitryon*) of mythological burlesque. We see characters motivated by youthful love, senile lust, selfless loyalty, selfish greed, affection, fear, modesty, vanity. Although farce abounds, it is super-

---

[1] See A. S. Gratwick, "Titus Maccius Plautus," *Classical Quarterly* 23 (1973): 78–84.

3

imposed on plays of basically sound construction and good characterization, and it is balanced by a sparkling gift of wit. If one quality above all others can be taken as Plautus' hallmark, it is his delight in language, manifested in constant puns, word coinages, alliteration, and assonance. Although the diction is colloquial, the comic idiom is enriched by countless rhetorical figures and is disciplined by Plautus' demanding verse forms. His rhythmical sense made him highly skillful in versification: in the *cantica* or lyric portions of his comedies, Plautus develops complex and sophisticated metrical patterns. His is an obtrusive style, seldom muted or subtle in its effect; but the undisguised verbal exuberance has been a strong feature in his perennial appeal.

Finally, then, we return to the question that has fascinated modern scholarship: if Plautine drama is an adaptation of Greek New Comedy, what is the precise nature of the Roman contribution? Can we possibly distinguish Greek and Roman strata?

Superficially, the impression is Greek. The *mise en scène* is always Greek (Athens, Ephesus, Thebes, or the like) and the characters usually have Greek names, of which the humorous etymologies would probably be lost on the majority of the Roman public. For most plays, moreover, the general dramatic structure is clearly derivative, as is much of the dialogue.

However, Plautus and his fellow playwrights were not constrained by academic reverence or servility: they were Italians, composing lively entertainment for the local comic stage. Smart wisecracks and scenes of tomfoolery were freely added. Characterization took on new colors. Most notable in this respect is the development and increased importance of the cunning slave, a brashly inventive character who was allowed by Roman comedians to dominate stage intrigue. It is virtually irrelevant to ask whether this slave is more "Italian," in a real historical sense, than his Greek counterpart. Plautus' interest was in theatrical effect, not in social validity. Still, at one level the dramatist does give us glimpses of an Italian reality underlying his comic world: both by inevitable accident and by humorous design, he is constantly introducing references to Roman legal, military, or religious institutions. Though it may seem incongruous for an Athenian courtesan to swear an oath by a Roman god or for a Greek slave to refer to service in the Roman army, Plautus' audience was not troubled by this fusion of two societies. His stage world has its own comic consistency and artistic reality. Above all, it has a stylistic unity derived from Plautus' controlled verse form and his rich Latin idiom.[2]

---

[2] Almost seventy years after it was first published, the most revered book in Plautine scholarship is still Eduard Fraenkel's *Plautinisches im Plautus* (Berlin, 1922), which developed

Roman Comedy on the Stage

We know a great deal about Greek theater production in classical and Hellenistic Athens, and we have good archaeological and literary evidence for the Roman theater of the late Republic and early Empire. In contrast, we are relatively ignorant of the manner in which the comedies of Plautus and Terence were originally produced during the creative half-century from 210 to 160 B.C. On most matters of stagecraft, we must depend on the textual evidence of the plays themselves.

The general circumstances of production can be stated with some confidence. The plays were presented at Rome, on the occasion of important public festivals or games (*ludi scaenici*). Attracted by the lure of free entertainment, huge audiences would throng to the festive outdoor site; there was no restriction of age, sex, or status. Some form of bench seating was clearly provided, although that point used to be a matter of scholarly dispute. Because there was no permanent theater—none would exist in Rome until 55 B.C.—an improvised stage was constructed for each festival. This stage was probably a long wooden platform (*pulpitum*), behind which was erected a makeshift wall to provide an appropriate backdrop, normally a street with two or three painted housefronts. The front doorways (*vestibula*) of these houses may have been framed with columns and a gabled roof. The house doors and the projecting wings at either end of the stage provided a variety of entrances and exits. Of the side entrances, that on stage left (to the audience's right) seems to have been viewed as the conventional route to the nearby town and the forum, whereas its counterpart on stage right (audience left) was seen as leading to the harbor, to the country, or to some other more remote locale.

Because of the dual heritage of Greek drama and popular Italian tradition, the Plautine stage had an abundance of conventions, features that strongly affected both technical production and acting style. Some of these might strike us as alien and exotic today, if we could somehow witness a Roman comedy in original performance; yet none, I feel, should create any barrier to understanding and enjoyment on the part of the modern reader. To begin with, the actors probably wore masks, each designed as a stylized caricature of the generic role. The question of masks has been a continuing controversy in Roman theatrical scholarship, but there is no good reason to doubt their use. Flamboyant wigs and colorful costumes were certainly the order of the

---

new and reliable criteria for identifying elements of Plautine originality. Fraenkel's pioneering study was revised and reissued as *Elementi Plautini in Plauto* (Florence, 1960), but has never been translated into English.

day: many passages in Plautus refer to the traditional, often bizarre appearance of such stock characters as the wily slave or the malevolent pimp. In addition, there were all-pervasive conventions of performance: Plautine comedy relied heavily on theatrical asides, simultaneous monologues, separate conversations, eavesdropping scenes, absurdly running slaves, and the like. Many actions and emotions, no doubt, were accompanied by highly stylized gestures that might amount to a code of communication between actor and audience.

A few of these apparently artificial devices—simultaneous monologues, for instance—may have been rendered more naturalistic by the extremely wide Roman stage; in the later permanent theaters, Roman stages could measure fifty meters or more from wing to wing. Many such conventions, however, can also be explained by the tendency (more pronounced in Plautus than in Terence) to adopt a thoroughly self-conscious attitude toward dramatic performance. The illusion of reality is not the ultimate goal in a theater that relishes interaction between actor and audience, a theater where glorious comic effects can be achieved by deliberate violation of the supposedly invisible fourth wall. In any event, artificial conventions within the dramaturgy of Plautus will not hinder a creative director today; on the contrary, they will soon be recognized as key ingredients in any effective production of a Plautine comedy.

I have seen Plautus presented successfully on a variety of modern stage configurations, from proscenium arch to theater-in-the-round. His comedies have such energy and strength that they do not have to be staged as museum pieces, with the original Roman conditions pedantically recreated. Like all true classics, they are eminently elastic and adaptable, provided that the humor is allowed to spring naturally and inevitably from the text. It is my conviction that they will work best with a minimum of tampering. Judicious abridgement may be desirable, since Plautus does have a tendency to be wordy and excessive. I doubt very much, however, that the plays will be rendered more accessible by adaptation or "modernization" of the text, nor are they likely to be improved by irrelevant stage business. A brisk pace is essential: an original Plautine performance might not have taken much longer than an hour.

It should be understood that our manuscripts of Roman comedy offer absolutely no guidance by way of stage directions. Obvious signals may be provided in the dialogue; for example, an actor will often herald an imminent entrance by referring to a creaking door. For more subtle clues, however, one must pay careful attention to the text. Some modern translators of Plautus try to address this problem by providing a plethora of stage directions (which often, admittedly, can be quite amusing in themselves). I have

MILES GLORIOSUS
(THE BRAGGART WARRIOR)

Introduction to *Miles Gloriosus*

Miles Gloriosus (*The Braggart Warrior*) was produced in 206 or 205 B.C., as we infer from a probable allusion to the contemporary comic poet Naevius (lines 211–212). Its model, we are told by the character Palaestrio, is an *Alazon* (*Braggart*) by an unnamed poet of Greek New Comedy. An immediate triumph at the time of its first production, Plautus' version has remained one of his most popular and influential comedies. Theatrical descendants of Pyrgopolynices[1] (the braggart) crowded the stages of the Renaissance: while England applauded Ralph Roister Doister, Bobadill, Don Armado, Pistol, and Sir John Falstaff, continental audiences were convulsed by a similar succession of bombastic soldier-heroes. Almost as important in the Renaissance tradition was the crafty servant, a generic character of whom Palaestrio was the prototype. Except perhaps for *Amphitryon,* no other comedy of Plautus has been more widely enjoyed and imitated.

For all its popular acclaim, *Miles Gloriosus* has been subject to attack by analytical scholars, who have been troubled by its division into two partly independent plot sequences. There is a real difficulty: after the brilliant introductory scene, the title character leaves the stage not to reappear until the play is two-thirds completed! This unusual structure, together with the evidence of several minor contradictions in plot detail, gave rise to the theory that Plautus' comedy was a fusion of two unconnected Greek originals. But it is a will-o'-the-wisp pursuit to try to reconstruct lost dramatic models

---

[1] There are good reasons to believe that Plautus invented many of his characters' names, especially those with humorous Greek etymologies. Pyrgopolynices means something like "Conqueror of Many Towers"; Artotrogus, "Breadmuncher"; Palaestrio, "Wrestler"; and Periplectomenus, "Embracer" or "Entangler." The *-ium* at the end of courtesans' names is derived from an affectionate Greek diminutive; Philocomasium means "Love a Party" and Acroteleutium "The Absolute End." We cannot tell how many members of Plautus' Roman audience knew enough Greek to appreciate these etymologies.

from extant imitations; and it then becomes risky, if not absurd, to use these reconstructions to criticize the existing play. The trend in modern scholarship is to conclude that Plautus chose to adapt a play that already contained a double plot—the gulling of the stupid slave and the more elegant deception of his vainglorious master.[2]

Certainly the Roman dramatist has tried to achieve a general comic unity: there is a consistency in theme, a balance in structure, and a coherence in character relationships. The braggart is the paradigm of self-deception, a man who has made fantasy a way of life. He occupies the ultimate comic position where absolute lack of self-knowledge creates a black-and-white contrast between appearance and reality. In the opening scene we merely sense the rich possibilities for comic reversal; before we are allowed to enjoy Pyrgopolynices' comeuppance, we are given a farcical lesson in human self-deception. Just as the stupid slave of Act Two is overthrown by a fatal trust in his physical eyesight, so, on a slightly higher plane, will the master be upended by a blind confidence in his total self-image. We can actually watch Plautus emphasize the superficial parallels in their respective predicaments so as to link the two deceptions and make the duping of Sceledrus a low-comedy pre-enactment of his master's downfall. Slave and master alike are brought to a position of groveling humiliation before the feet of a neutral bystander, the neighbor Periplectomenus, who gives mock-serious acquittal to each.

The greatest force for unity and the pivotal dramatic character is the master craftsman of intrigue, the slave hero Palaestrio. No other characterization offers better evidence of Plautus' creativity and comic genius; for we have reason to believe that these larger-than-life slave roles were mainly the product of the Roman stage. The élan, the poise, the fantastic and ebullient diction, the improbable imagery—all of this is vintage Plautus. We see, for example, the brilliant incongruity of the slave who exercises absolute authority over all free men whose lives he touches. (As we are told repeatedly, he is the *imperator,* the supreme commanding general.) Although Plautus indicates no serious didactic purpose, he may suggest through Palaestrio that self-knowledge, however cynically applied, confers a freedom of action that transcends personal status. In the looking-glass world of comedy, the slave becomes the heroic warrior, while the braggart follows him in blind servility. A sort of slave-nonslave, Palaestrio wins the promise of freedom from both his masters. His triumphant emancipation is comic proof that he rules an island of sanity in a vast sea of pretense and self-delusion.

---

[2]See Gordon Williams, "Evidence for Plautus' Workmanship in the Miles Gloriosus," *Hermes* 86 (1958): 79–105. The problem is examined at enormous length by Lothar Schaaf, *Der Miles Gloriosus des Plautus und sein griechisches Original* (Munich: Fink, 1977).

Miles Gloriosus was my first experience in translating Plautine comedy for stage production: in the main, this version dates from 1966. Although I believe that I would do things rather differently today, I have decided to make only a few minor corrections and revisions, thus avoiding obvious inconsistencies of style.

The most readily accessible edition and commentary on the play is Mason Hammond, Arthur M. Mack, and Walter Moskalew, *T. Macci Plauti Miles Gloriosus,* 2d edition (Cambridge, Mass.: Harvard University Press, 1970).

CHARACTERS

PYRGOPOLYNICES	a vainglorious soldier, resident in Ephesus
ARTOTROGUS	his parasite
PALAESTRIO	a cunning slave of Pyrgopolynices'
PLEUSICLES	a young Athenian; Palaestrio's former master
PHILOCOMASIUM	a young Athenian courtesan; Pyrgopolynices' concubine, in love with Pleusicles
SCELEDRUS	a stupid slave of Pyrgopolynices'; Philocomasium's guard
PERIPLECTOMENUS	a pleasant old man; Pleusicles' host in Ephesus
ACROTELEUTIUM	a courtesan; client of Periplectomenus'
MILPHIDIPPA	her alluring maid
LURCIO	a bibulous slave of Pyrgopolynices'
CARIO	a bloodthirsty cook of Periplectomenus'
YOUNG SLAVE	an unnamed slave of Periplectomenus'
ATTENDANT SLAVES	minor or silent roles

ACT I

The stage represents a street, ostensibly in Ephesus, but in fact not unlike a typical street in Rome. We see two houses, side by side. Although they are attached to each other by a common wall, it is clear that they are two distinct residences. The house on stage left belongs to Pyrgopolynices, the braggart warrior; its neighbor belongs to Periplectomenus, an urbane and elderly bachelor. Each house has a prominent door opening onto the street. Downstage center there is a low altar; otherwise the street is clear.

Enter PYRGOPOLYNICES, *preceded by several weird and dismally incompetent slaves; he is followed at a short distance by his parasite* ARTOTROGUS, *who is well fed and well oiled.*

Act I, Scene 1

Pyrgo.   (*striking a pose and addressing his slaves*)
Shine my shield till it glows and glitters and gleams
Like the radiant rays of the sun from a summer sky;
So, when its hour has come and the foe's at hand,
Its dazzling light will dizzy the enemy line.
My task will be to comfort this pining sword: 5
My gay blade mustn't despair or get down in the mouth.
Poor lad, he's lived so long with his nose in my belt
That now he longs to give someone a belt in the nose.
Where's Artotrogus?

Artot.   Here, beside a hero
Audacious, tenacious, sagacious; good gracious, a *king*!   10
And a warrior! Even Mars would hesitate
To match his deeds of courage against yours.

Pyrgo.   Who was that man I saved on Cockroach Plains,
Where the commander-in-chief was Neptune's grandson,
Bumbomachides Clutomestoridysarchides?   15

19

Artot. I remember. The one with golden armor,
Whose troops you puffed apart with a breath of air,
As the wind blows leaves or scatters a house of straw.

Pyrgo. Great Pollux, that was nothing.

Artot.   Great Hercules,
It was nothing compared to other deeds
I could describe—(*aside*) except you never did them.   20
(*speaking directly to the audience*)
If anyone knows a more colossal liar,
A man more stuffed with pride and vanity,
Then call me your slave; I'll put myself on the block.
Why do I stay? His cheese sauce is divine!

Pyrgo. Where are you?

Artot.   Here, sir. Remember, sir,
That poor elephant we met in India?   25
You forcefully flung your fist and fractured his arm!

Pyrgo. His "arm"?

Artot.   I actually meant to say his "leg."

Pyrgo. But I hit him a careless blow.

Artot.   By Pollux, if only
You'd really tried, you'd have transpenetrated your arm
Through hide and guts clear down to elephant marrow.   30

Pyrgo. Let's not discuss it now.

Artot.   Heavens to Hercules,
It's a waste of valuable breath for you to tell me:
I know what a great, strong man you are.
(*aside*) This painful role is strictly from hunger, friends:
I've got to get an earful to keep my stomach cheerful,
So I'm forced to nod my head to all his lies.   35

Pyrgo. Now what was I saying?

Artot.	Aha! I know what you want
	To say. It's a fact, sir, you did! I remember, you did!

Pyrgo. Did what?

Artot. Well, whatever it was that you did.

Pyrgo. Have you got—

Artot. Wax tablets? Yes, and a stylus, too.

Pyrgo. How intelligent of you to read my mind!

Artot. I'm a student of all your ways; that's only right.   40
My mission is to sniff your every whim.

Pyrgo. How good's your memory?

Artot. (*madly improvising*) In Cilicia, I recall,
A hundred and fifty, a hundred in Babblebaloneya,
Thirty Sards, three score from Macedon—
All men that you . . . killed off one afternoon.   45

Pyrgo. And what's the total sum?

Artot. (*after a rapid mental calculation*) Seven thousand.

Pyrgo. That should be right. First-class arithmetic!

Artot. It's not written down, but I still remember it.

Pyrgo. Great Pollux, I love your memory!

Artot. It runs on food.

Pyrgo. If you never change, you'll never miss a meal;   50
You'll always be my table's closest friend.

Artot. (*with renewed enthusiasm*)
In Cappadocia, five hundred at once (if your sword
Had not gone dull) you'd have slain with a single slice.

Pyrgo.   Poor nonentities, I let them live.

Artot.   Why should I tell you what every mortal knows?   55
    Pyrgopolynices, you alone on earth
    In courage and beauty and action stand invincible.
    All the girls adore you, naturally,
    Because you're so handsome. Yesterday some of them
    Caught me by the sleeve.

Pyrgo.   And what did they say?   60

Artot.   They grilled me. "Is he Achilles?" said one to me.
    "No," I replied; "his brother." Then the second
    Said, "Merciful Castor, what a gorgeous man!
    A real gentleman! Look at his dreamy hair!
    I envy the girls that climb into bed with him!"   65

Pyrgo.   That's what they said?

Artot.   Didn't they both implore me
    To march you past on parade over there today?

Pyrgo.   It's a pain to be painfully handsome.

Artot.   You're telling me.
    The girls are pests: they plead and badger and beg
    To see you, ordering me to bring you round.   70
    I can't attend to your business affairs.

Pyrgo.   I think it's time for us to go to the forum,
    Where I ought to pay the salary
    Of those recruits I signed up yesterday.
    King Seleucus is awfully keen for me   75
    To round up and enlist recruits for him.
    (*solemnly*) This day is dedicated to the king.

Artot.   Let's go then, sir.

Pyrgo.   Follow on, attendant lords.
    (*They march out toward the forum, stage left.*)

ACT II

The door of the house on stage left opens, and PALAESTRIO *steps forward to address the audience. Although he is Pyrgopolynices' slave, his prior loyalty is to the young Athenian Pleusicles, as he will explain.* PALAESTRIO *is ingratiating and shrewd, a paragon of the tricky slave.*

Act II, Scene 1

Palae.   To tell you the plot of our play is my kind intention,
       If you'll be so good as to listen with total attention.   80
       If you're not in the mood, get up and go out for a walk;
       Make room for someone who wants to hear me talk.
       (*a defiant pause*)
       So you'll know why you're present in this place of joy,
       I'll tell you the name and the plot (a thumbnail sketch)
       Of the comedy that we're about to play.   85
       In Greek it's called *Alazon* (or *The Braggart*);
       Our Latin title is *Miles Gloriosus.*
       This town is Ephesus. That soldier is my master—
       He's on his way to the forum: boastful, shameless,
       Slimy, full of lies and lechery.   90
       He says the girls all chase him, out of control;
       The truth is, he's a laughingstock wherever he goes.
       Our hookers pucker up to egg him on,
       Their every smooch a smirk of ridicule.
       I haven't been his faithful slave for long.   95
       I want you to know the story—how I came
       From my old service into this new servility.
       Pay attention! Now I'll begin to weave the plot.

       I had a master in Athens, a fine young man;
       He was hot for a harlot (maid-in-Athens brand)   100
       And she loved him—a romantic situation.

He was sent to Naupactus as an ambassador
On behalf of our great and glorious government.
Meanwhile, this soldier comes along to Athens,
And snakes his way in beside my master's girl.   105
He went ahead by playing up to her mother
With baubles and bottles of bubbly and fabulous food.
Soon the old girl and the soldier were thick as thieves.
The moment our soldier saw his golden chance,
He bamboozled that bitch—the mother of the girl   110
My master loved; for unbeknownst to mom
He whisked her daughter off to a boat and brought her
Here to Ephesus, against her will.

When I knew my master's girl was filched from Athens,
Quick as a wink I got hold of a ship myself,   115
And set out for Naupactus to bring my master the news.
But when we were far at sea, as luck would have it,
Pirates seized the boat I was sailing on.
I had no chance; the message never arrived.
They gave me as a present to this soldier.   120

After he brought me home into his household,
I saw my master's love, the Athenian girl.
When she caught sight of me, she winked and gave a sign
Not to speak her name; then, when the chance arose,
Upon my shoulder poured out her tale of woe: 125
She told me she longed to fly from here to Athens,
Said she still loved my young Athenian master,
And hated no one worse than that soldier of ours.

As for me, when I learned the woman's heart,
I scribbled a message, signed it, secretly   130
Passed it to a certain merchant to take to Athens
To my master, who'd loved this girl, in order to tell him
To come here. He didn't ignore my note;
You see, he's come, and is staying here next door
With a close friend of the family, a charming old man.   135
This old man's trying to help his love-struck guest;
He's pitching in with advice and encouragement.

And so, inside, I've hit on a staggering stunt
For the lovers to have a private rendezvous.

24

The soldier had given a room to his little lady,   140
Her own retreat—no one else allowed inside—
And in that room I chopped a hole in the wall
To grant her secret access to this house;
The old man knows I did it: he gave advice.

I've got a fellow slave—a worthless type;   145
The soldier ordered *him* to guard the girl.
With the help of a slick sort of confidence trick
And a clever disguise, we'll throw dust in his eyes!
We'll make the man unsee what he plainly saw.
Don't get confused: today this woman will play   150
Two roles as she passes back and forth. She'll be
One and the same girl, whatever she may pretend.
With her help we'll make an ass of the slave on guard.

I hear a noise from the old man's house next door.
That's him: the charming old man I told you about.   155

Act II, Scene 2

The old man PERIPLECTOMENUS *emerges through the door of his own house, stage right. He is furiously berating his slaves.*

Perip.   From this time on, by Hercules,
        If you see a stranger up on the roof,
        And let him escape without broken bones,
        I'll cut you to pieces! I'll skin you alive!

        My neighbors here have a grandstand view
        Of all that's happening in my house:
        They simply peer through the open skylight!

        Here's my public proclamation:
        If you see any man from that soldier's house
        Cavorting or sporting on top of our roof   160
        (Except Palaestrio, of course),
        Then give him a shove down into the street.
        Whether he claims to be chasing a chicken,
        Pursuing a pigeon or hunting a monkey,
        All you slaves are as good as dead

Unless you pummel and pound him to pulp.
And while you're at it, check that house
For any infraction of gambling laws;
If they've been rolling dice, make sure
They've got no bones to party with.   165

Palae.   Some kind of crime has been committed,
By a man from our house—this much I've heard;
And so the old man's told his boys
To fracture all my fellow slaves.
But I heard him say he didn't mean me;
Who gives a damn what he does to the rest?
I'll go up to him.

Perip.   Who's this?
Is that you coming, Palaestrio?

Palae.   What's going on, Periplectomenus?

Perip.   You're just the man I want to see.   170

Palae.   What is it? Why are you ranting and roaring
Against our house?

Perip.   Our goose is cooked!

Palae.   What's the trouble?

Perip.   It's out in the open.

Palae.   What's out in the open?

Perip.   From the roof
A moment ago some man looked down—
One of the people who live in your house—
And through our skylight caught a glimpse
Of Philocomasium and my young guest   175
Kissing each other.

Palae.   Who was the man?

Perip.   Your fellow slave.

Palae.   Which one do you mean?

Perip.   I've no idea: he took to his heels
In a hell of a hurry.

Palae.   I've a hunch
It's all over with me.

Perip.   When he ran, I bellowed:
"Hey, what are you doing up there on the roof?"
He shouted back without slowing down;
He said he was on a monkey chase.

Palae.   Ye gods, to think my life's been ruined
All on account of a wandering ape!   180
Look, is the girl Philocomasium still here
In your house?

Perip.   When I came out, she was.

Palae.   Please go, tell her to cross to our house
Quick as she can, and let the whole household
See her at home, unless she wants
Her love affair to give all us slaves
A swinging party up on the cross.

Perip.   I've told her that; if you've nothing to add—

Palae.   But I have. You've got to tell her this: 185
On no account must she lose her grip
On woman's instinctive genius;
And she must cultivate all the acquired
Skills of her sex.

Perip.   How do you mean?

Palae.   To confute that confounded spy on the roof
And convince him he couldn't have seen her there.
What if he's seen her a hundred times—
She must deny it all the same.
     She's got good looks and a treacherous tongue,
     She's brash and bold and brassy;

27

She trusts herself, she can lean on herself,
She's sneaky and snake-in-the-grass-y.
Let her face her accuser and talk him down
By swearing a solemn and sacred oath.   190
She's well supplied with lies and perjuries,
Fibs and frauds and fabrications,
Diabolical machinations,
Hypocritical falsifications.
   A slippery woman needn't shop
For fresh chicanery at the store;
Her garden at home produces a crop
Of lies by the bushel beside her door.

Perip.   If she's here, I'll pass the message.
What do you think, Palaestrio?   195
What trick are you tossing now in your brain?

Palae.   Just keep quiet a little while,
While I muster all my plans,
While I ponder what to do,
While I think of a wily trick
To dupe my wily fellow slave,
Who saw her kissing here just now.
I'll make him unsee what he saw.

Perip.   Ponder away! I'll back off
To give you room. (*to audience*) Just look at the man!   200
The way he stands with his face screwed up,
Stern and worried and full of thought!
He knocks on his head with his fist. I think
He's calling his brain to come out and join in.

Look! He's turning; his left hand now
Is propped in position on his left leg,
While his right hand acts as an adding machine,
Pounding out sums on the other leg.
Ouch! What a slap! This infant plan
Is having a dreadfully difficult birth.   205

He's snapped his fingers; he's working away;
He's shifting position again and again.

Oh, look now! He shakes his head:
He doesn't seem to like what he's found.
Whatever comes out, it'll be well done:
He'll never produce a half-baked plan.

Hey! Now he's entered the building trade:
He's propped a column under his chin.
Go on! I take no pleasure at all
In that kind of architectural style: 210
I've heard of a poet—a foreign type—
Who holds a similar propped-up pose,
While languishing inside the lockup,
Doubly guarded all day long.[3]

Ah, how pretty! He's standing there gracefully,
Just like a slave in a comedy.
He'll never get a moment's rest
Until he gains his heart's desire.
I think he's found it.

| Palae. | (adopting an attitude of self-harangue)[4] |
| | Come! if you've got it, |

Wake up, don't let yourself fall asleep,   215
Unless you want to do sentry duty,
Bruised and battered and black and blue.
I'm speaking to *you*. Have you been drinking?
Hey! I'm talking to you, Palaestrio!
Come on, wake up! Come on, get up!
Come on, *it's morning*!

(replying to the voice of his alter ego) I hear you.

(first voice continues)
You see? The enemy's close at hand;

---

[3] One of Plautus' rare topical jokes, this is apparently a jibe at the Roman poet Naevius, who had been imprisoned for his lampoons.

[4] In the following passage (lines 215–232), I have departed from the assignment of speeches found in the manuscripts, preferring the attractive proposal of Eduard Fraenkel in *Museum Helveticum* 25 (1968): 231–234. In his book *Plautus in Performance* (Princeton, 1985), pp. 21–24, Niall W. Slater suggests that a similar "internal dialogue" in *Epidicus* might actually have been staged as a conversation between the actor and his mask.

Your back is under siege; take thought!
Bring in reinforcements; summon aid.
It's time for haste; no time to waste.   220
Take the offensive! Some way, somehow,
Circle and cut them off in the rear!
Lay down a blockade to foil the foe,
Put up a stockade to guard our men.
Destroy the enemy's line of supply,
Then build a road that will make it safe
For food and provisions and army divisions
To be transported wherever you go.
Look after this business! It calls for speed.   225
Come on, be quick, be calm, be cool,
Produce and perfect a practical plan
To force the seen to become unseen
And make what's done come all undone.

Perip.   (*to audience*) This fellow's launching a great campaign,
           He's building bulging battlements.

Palae.   Just give the word that you'll take charge,
           And our hearts will soar with hope that we
           Can crush our enemies.

Perip.   Here's the word: 230
           I'll take charge.

Palae.   I say you'll get
           Whatever you're after.

Perip.   Jupiter
           Bless you, friend! Could you please
           Let me share in your bold invention?

Palae.   Shhh!
           I'll lead you into the secret realm
           Of dark skulduggery. Soon you'll know
           My plans as well as I do myself.

Perip.   I promise they'll be safe with me.

Palae.   My boss—this soldier—hasn't got human

Skin; he's surrounded with elephant hide.   235
And no more brains than a pile of rocks.

Perip. I won't argue with you on this!

Palae. Here's the scheme I've got in mind;
I'm contemplating a pleasant plot.
I'll tell him that Philocomasium's sister
(I'll say that she's an identical twin)
Has just arrived in town from Athens,
Bringing along her fiancé.
As like her sister as peas in a pod!
And I'll tell him they're both staying as guests   240
Here in your house.

Perip.   Magnificent!
Delightful! A spectacular invention!

Palae. As a result, if my fellow slave
Brings a charge before the soldier
And claims he's seen her over here,
Kissing a stranger, I'll calmly prove
It was really her sister the fellow saw
Hugging and kissing her lover.

Perip.   Superb!   245
I'll tell the same story if the soldier
Questions me.

Palae.   But be sure to say
They're identical; and Philocomasium
Must be forewarned, so she won't slip
When the soldier questions her.

Perip.   Brilliant!
But say if the soldier gets the urge
To see them both, hand in hand,
What then?

Palae.   That's easy. Anyone clever
Can bang together a thousand excuses: 250
    "She's not at home, she's out for a walk,

31

      She's doing her face, she's taking a nap,
      She's in the tub, she's at supper, she's busy.
      She hasn't the time—too bad, old chap."
      You can put him off as much as you want,
      If only we're careful, right at the start,
      To make him believe our lies are true.

Perip.   A lovely plan!

Palae.   Please go in, then,
      And tell the woman, if she's there,   255
      To cross to our house at once. And look—
      Teach her, train her, school her well
      To use our plan the way we wove it:
      She's her twin sister.

Perip.   I'll send her home
      Schooled like a scholar. Anything else?

Palae.   Just go in.

Perip.   I'm going. (*exit into his own house*)

Palae.   It's home
      For me too: I've got a man to track.
      I'll go under cover and snoop around,   260
      To find out which of my fellow slaves
      Was chasing a monkey over the roof.
      The man would be bound to spread the word
      That he'd seen our master's light-of-love
      Here, next door, in the fond embrace
      Of some young punk from out of town.
      I know the type: "Have I got *news*!
      I've got to tell someone before I burst!"   265

      If I learn who saw her, he'll be faced
      With catapults and battering rams.
      My plans are ready, my aim is fixed:
      To storm his camp and seize the man.
      If I can't find him, I'll follow my nose
      And sniff his tracks like a hungry hound
      Until I've chased the fox to his den.

Listen! Our doors are creaking open;
I'd better lower my voice a bit.   270
A fellow slave is coming out;
This man is Philocomasium's guard.

Act II, Scene 3

Enter SCELEDRUS *through the door of the soldier's house. Palaestrio's fellow slave is not very bright.*

Scele. Unless I've just been having a nightmare,
Walking around on top of the roof,
Honest to Pollux I'd swear I saw
Philocomasium, master's girl friend,
Here, next door, up to no good.

Palae. He's the one who saw her kissing—
I've heard him say that much himself.   275

Scele. Who's that?

Palae.   Your fellow slave. What is it,
Sceledrus?

Scele.   Oh, Palaestrio,
I'm so happy to see you!

Palae.   Why?
What's the trouble? Give me a clue.

Scele. I'm afraid—

Palae.   Of what?

Scele.   O Herc! I'm afraid
That today all the slaves in our house
Will get lifted up to hang from the cross.

Palae. Go lift yourself! I don't much care
For these uplifting thoughts of yours.   280

33

Scele.	Probably you don't know the amazing Thing that has just happened in here.
Palae.	What thing do you mean?
Scele.	It's wicked and awful!
Palae.	Keep it to yourself, then. Don't tell me; I've no desire to know.
Scele.	Well, I won't allow you not to know. Today I chased our little monkey Over onto this man's roof.
Palae.	Great Pollux, Sceledrus, why in the world Would a chimp be chased by a chump like you?
Scele.	Oh, go to hell!
Palae.	Well, my advice To you, my friend, is go—on speaking.
Scele.	As luck would have it, through the skylight I looked down to the house next door. There I saw Philocomasium kissing Some young fellow I didn't know.
Palae.	Sceledrus! A scandalous, slanderous lie!
Scele.	I definitely saw her.
Palae.	You?
Scele.	Yes, me. I saw her with these two eyes of mine.
Palae.	Go on, you didn't! A likely story!
Scele.	Do you think there's something wrong with my eyes?
Palae.	I don't give medical advice.

285

290

34

But if the gods are on your side,
You'll have the sense to drop that tale.
I warn you not to lose your head:
You might not get it back again.
Unless you stop that stupid talk
A double death's in store for you.   295

Scele.   Why do you say double?

Palae.   I'll explain.
In the first case, if you falsely charge
Our Philocomasium, you're a goner!
In the second, if your facts are right
And you were the guard, you're a goner again.

Scele.   I don't know what'll become of me:
I only know I really saw it.

Palae.   Do you still insist, you idiot?

Scele.   What
Do you want me to say except what I saw?   300
Anyhow, she's still inside right here,
At the house next door.

Palae.   What, not at home?

Scele.   Take a look, go inside yourself;
I don't ask you to take my word.

Palae.   All right, I'll go. (*exit into soldier's house*)

Scele.   I'll wait for you here.
(*to audience*) While I'm at it, I'll set a trap;
I'll catch that heifer and tan her hide,
As soon as she tries to return to the barn.

What am I going to do? The soldier
Put me in charge of guarding her.   305
If I accuse her now, I'm through;
I'm through all the same if I shut up
And the news gets out. What in the world's

More shameless and depraved than women?
While I was up on the roof, that girl
Just left her room and went outside.
Pollux! What a brazen bitch!
If the soldier finds this out,
I swear to Herc he'll hang the house
And hoist yours truly on the cross.   310
Whatever happens, I'll keep mum
Rather than die in agony.
How can I possibly guard a woman
Who's always got herself for sale?

Palae.   (*emerging from the soldier's house*)
Sceledrus, Sceledrus, what other man
Is such a barefaced liar as you?
When you were born the gods above
Must've groaned with anger!

Scele.   What is it?

Palae.   Do you want to get your eyes gouged out,
When they're seeing things that don't exist?   315

Scele.   That don't exist?

Palae.   I wouldn't buy
Your claim to life for a worm-eaten walnut!

Scele.   What's the trouble?

Palae.   What's the trouble,
You're asking me?

Scele.   Why not ask you?

Palae.   Wouldn't it be a good idea
To get your tattletale tongue cut out?

Scele.   My what?

Palae.   Look! Philocomasium's

36

At home—the girl you saw next door,
Kissing and hugging another man.   320

Scele.   I'm surprised you can't afford
To drink a better grade of wine.

Palae.   Come again?

Scele.   There's something wrong with your eyes.

Palae.   Well, as for you, my squinting friend,
You're blind: that's all that's wrong with *your* eyes.
That woman's definitely at home.

Scele.   At home, you say?

Palae.   At home, I say.

Scele.   You're pulling my leg, Palaestrio.

Palae.   Then I'd better go home and wash my hands.

Scele.   How's that?

Palae.   'Cause you're a muddy mess.   325

Scele.   You go to hell!

Palae.   You'll go to hell,
Sceledrus, I promise you,
Unless you get a new pair of eyes
And learn to sing another tune.
But look! Our door is opening here.

Scele.   (*indicating Periplectomenus' house*)
Well, *this* is the door I'm looking at;
There's no way that she can cross
From here to here, except by the door.

Palae.   Look! She's home! Oh, Sceledrus,
Some bee in your bonnet is bugging you.   330

Scele.   I see for myself, I think for myself,
I trust myself more than anyone else:
No man is going to frighten me off
From knowing she's inside this house.
I'll plant myself here, in case that girl
Crawls to her home while I'm off guard.

Palae.   (*aside*) I've got him now; I'll whirl him about
And hurl him down from his towering fort.
(*to* SCELE.) Do you want me to try to make you admit
You're feeble-sighted?

Scele.   Go ahead and try.   335

Palae.   That you haven't got a brain in your head—
That your eyes are useless?

Scele.   That I'd love!

Palae.   I believe you said our master's girl
Was over here?

Scele.   Yes. Furthermore,
I say I saw her playing around,
Inside the house, with another man.

Palae.   You know there isn't a passageway
From here to our house.

Scele.   Yes, I know.

Palae.   No balcony or garden route
Unless you fly through the skylight.

Scele.   I know.   340

Palae.   Well then, if she's home, and if
I make you see her leaving our house,
Have you earned a thumping?

Scele.   All right.

Palae.   Watch that door. Don't let her sneak out
        Secretly to cross this way.

Scele.   That's just my plan.

Palae.   I'll soon produce
        Her here, in person, on the street.
                  (exit again into soldier's house)

Scele.   Go ahead and try. I want to know
        Whether I saw what I think I saw,   345
        Or whether he'll do what he says he'll do
        To prove the girl is really home.
        The eyes I've got are perfectly good,
        I'm not in the market for any more.

        This fellow's always sniffing around,
        He's always playing up to her;
        He's the first to be called to dinner,
        He's the first to be given a bite;
        He's been in our house for just three years,   350
        Yet no one else within our walls
        Wallows in greater luxury.

        But I'd better do what I've got to do:
        I'll just stand and watch this door.
        I'll guard it this way. Here's one time
        That no one'll make a fool of me.

        (SCELEDRUS *stations himself in front of the old man's house, facing the*
        audience. From Palaestrio's crucifixion taunt in the next scene, we can
        assume that he stands with his arms spread out to block the door.)

Act II, Scene 4

PALAESTRIO *and* PHILOCOMASIUM *emerge stealthily from the soldier's house.*

Palae.   *(sotto voce)* Obey your orders; don't forget.

Philo.   Stop nagging; you surprise me.

Palae.   Well, I'm afraid you're not too bright.

Philo.   Give me ten empty-headed girls   355
Without a scheming thought among them:
I'll train them and still have tricks to spare.
Come on, get on with your clever games.
I'll move away from you a little.

Palae.   (*aloud*) What do you say, Sceledrus?

Scele.   I'm busy here. I've ears, just speak your wishes.

Palae.   I suspect you're doomed to die
Outside the gate, in that position:
Hands spread out and nailed to the crossbar.

Scele.   Why in the world do you think that?   360

Palae.   Look to your left. Who is that woman?

Scele.   *Holy heavenly gods almighty!*
This is master's concubine!

Palae.   That's my own opinion, too.
Come on now, since you're so eager—

Scele.   What shall I do?

Palae.   Prepare to die.

Philo.   Where's that honest slave of yours
Who was spreading ugly libelous lies
About poor little me?

Palae.   Here you are!
He told *me* what *I* told *you*.   365

Philo.   You big crook, do you claim you saw
Me here next door, in the act of kissing?

Palae.   "With some unknown young fellow," he said.

Scele. That's what I said, by Hercules!

Philo. *You* saw *me*?

Scele. With my very own eyes!
I think—

Philo. —You won't have those eyes for long,
If they see more than there is to see.

Scele. So help me Herc, you'll never stop me
From having seen what I said I saw.

Philo. Really, it's not very bright of me   370
To stand and chat with this lunatic:
I'll merely have him put to death.

Scele. Threaten away! I'm sure the cross
Will be my final resting place.
All my family settled there:
Great-grandfather, Grandpa, Dad.
Just the same, these threats of yours
Can't do a thing to hurt my eyes.
But I'd like a word or two with you,
Palaestrio. (*to* PALAE., *sotto voce*) I want to know,   375
Where did she come from?

Palae. Where else but home?

Scele. Home?

Palae. Am I standing here?

Scele. I think so.
It's simply amazing how she can move:
There she *was*; here she *is* . . . where she *wasn't*!
I know there's no balcony on our house,
There's no garden route to cross by,
There's no window that isn't barred.
(*He turns to* PHILOCOMASIUM.)
Damn it, I *did* see you inside here.

Palae.	Hold on, you scoundrel, are you still trying To accuse this woman?

Philo.   Merciful Castor,   380
I think my dream has just come true—
A dream I had this very night.

Palae.   What did you dream?

Philo.   I'll tell you now.
Pay very close attention, please.
Last night as I slept, I seemed to learn
That my dear sister—she's my twin—
Had come from Athens to Ephesus,
Bringing her lover along with her.
Both of them, it seemed to me,
Had come to stay in this house next door.   385

Palae.   (*aside*) The story you hear is really Palaestrio's
Dream. (*aloud*) Go on, continue.

Philo.   My sister's arrival had made me happy,
So it seemed; but on her account
I felt I was heavily weighted down
With a load of grave suspicion.
For one of my household seemed to me,
In my sleep, to be accusing me
(Exactly as you're doing now)
Of having kissed some strange young man,   390
Because that sister of mine (my twin)
Had kissed her very own dear love.
I was the victim, so I dreamt,
Of such a false and groundless charge.

Palae.   (*with reverent awe*)
And now you're awake, the same events
Are happening as you saw in your sleep?
Sweet Hercules! A dream come true!
Go inside and pray to the gods.
I feel we must relate this news
To the soldier.

Philo.	That's what I intend; 395
	I certainly could never bear
	To be slandered with immorality.
	(exit into the soldier's house)

Scele.   I'm a little afraid of what I've done;
I've got an itch all over my back.

Palae.   Do you know you're finished?

Scele.   *(bemused)* Now, at least,
She's certainly home. My mind's made up
To guard our doorway now, right here,
Wherever *she* is.

Palae.   Sceledrus, hey!
How strangely similar her dream
To the pattern you revealed in life,   400
When you suspected you saw her kissing!

Scele.   I don't know what I should believe.
It's reached the point that what I've seen
I no longer think I really saw.

Palae.   Great Herc, it'll be too late, I think,
When you come to. If this news gets
To our master first, you're sweetly screwed.

Scele.   Now I've got the funny feeling
I'm walking around inside a fog.   405

Palae.   Obviously that was true just now
Since she was home here all the time.

Scele.   I really don't know what to say.
I didn't see her, and yet I did.

Palae.   Honest to Pollux, you're such a fool
I think you've almost ruined us:
Wanting to play the faithful slave
For master, you've almost been swallowed up.

43

But listen! That was a creaking sound
From our neighbor's door. I'll keep quiet.   410

Act II, Scene 5

PHILOCOMASIUM *appears from the old man's house, hastily disguised as her twin sister. Her attitude is melodramatically reverent and gravely heroic.*

Philo.   Fire the altar! Praise and joy!
I thank thee, Diana of Ephesus!
O incense, arise to her in the skies,
O sweet-smoke odor of Araby.
Yea, when I rode in the realm of Neptune,
Tossed by the tempest's turbulent tide,
She saved me—saved me from sore affliction,
While the baleful billows boiled.

Scele.   Palaestrio, O Palaestrio!

Palae.   O Sceledrus, Sceledrus, what is it?   415

Scele.   This woman, who's just come out from here,
Is she our master's concubine,
Philocomasium, or isn't she?

Palae.   By heaven, I think so; yes, she seems so.
But it's simply amazing how she can move:
There she *was*; here she *is* . . . where she *wasn't!*
(If it's her.)

Scele.   Have you got any doubt
That this is her?

Palae.   She seems to be.

Scele.   Let's go near, let's speak her name.
Hey there, Philocomasium!   420
What business have you in that house,
And what're you up to over there?
Why are you silent? I'm talking to you!

Palae.   No, by Pollux, you're all on your own,
This girl is making no reply.

Scele.   I'm talking to *you,* you sneaky slut,
Who wander around the neighborhood.

Philo.   (*icily*) With whom are you conversing?

Scele.   With *whom*? With *youm*!

Philo.   But who are you,
And what have you got to do with me?   425

Scele.   You ask me who I am?

Philo.   Why not?
Why shouldn't I ask what I don't know?

Palae.   Who am I, then, if you don't know him?

Philo.   You're an awful nuisance, whoever you are,
Both you and he.

Scele.   You don't know us?

Philo.   Neither of you.

Scele.   Oh dear, I'm afraid—

Palae.   Afraid of what?

Scele.   Afraid that somewhere
We've lost our own identity!
She says she doesn't know you or me.

Palae.   I want to follow this up, Sceledrus,   430
(Whether we're us or someone else):
It could be that a neighbor of ours,
While we were looking the other way,
Has made some change in you and me.

Scele.   Damn it, I'm certainly me!

Palae. And I
Am I. You're looking for trouble, wench!
I'm speaking to you. Hey! Philocomasium!

Philo. What's got into your crazy mind
That you make up silly names to call me? 435

Palae. Aha! And what are you normally called?

Philo. My name's Justine.[5]

Scele. Like hell it is!
To trick us, Philocomasium,
You want to have a made-up name.
You're not Justine, you're *un*-Justine,
And you're out to do my master harm.

Philo. I?

Scele. Yes, you.

Philo. Who yesterday
Came from Athens to Ephesus,
Just at nightfall, with my lover,
A young Athenian?

Palae. Tell me, please, 440
What's your business in Ephesus?

Philo. My dear twin sister I heard was living
Here; I've come to find her.

Scele. Slut!

Philo. Well, I swear to Castor, I'm a fool
To talk with you. I'm leaving now.

Scele. But I don't intend to let you leave.

---

[5]Philocomasium dubs her twin sister "Dicea," a Latin version of the Greek *Dikaia* ("Just Lady"). Sceledrus retorts that she is not Dicea but Adicea.

Philo.	Let go!
Scele.	Ah, no! You're caught in the act.
	I won't let go.
Philo.	You'll get a slap like a thunderclap 445
	If you don't let go!
Scele.	(*to* PALAE., *who hasn't moved*) Damn it, get with it!
	Hold her by the other arm.
Palae.	I'm not anxious to have my back
	Exposed to trouble. For all I know
	She may not be Philocomasium
	But another woman just like her.
Philo.	Will you let me go or won't you?
Scele.	No!
	By force and strength, against your will,
	If you won't come gladly, I'll drag you home.
Philo.	This is my home, when I'm abroad; 450
	My real home base is back in Athens.
	I don't care for that home of yours,
	And I don't know who you people are.
Scele.	Get a lawyer and sue me! I'll never release you
	Unless you give your solemn pledge
	That, if I do, you'll go inside.
Philo.	You're forcing me, whoever you are.
	I give my pledge: let me go, and then
	I'll go inside where you command. 455
Scele.	All right, you're free.
Philo.	All right, I'm gone!
	(*exit into the old man's house*)
Scele.	There's a woman's word for you!

Palae.   Sceledrus, you've let our prize
Slip through your fingers. There's no doubt
That she's our master's concubine.
Do you want to give this all you've got?

Scele.   What should I do?

Palae.   Bring me a sword
Out here.

Scele.   What will you do with it?

Palae.   (*heroically*) First I'll burst into the house:
If I've spied a man inside   460
Kissing Philocomasium,
I'll lop off his head—and he'll be dead!

Scele.   Did it seem to be her?

Palae.   Great Pollux, yes,
Without a doubt.

Scele.   But oh, the way
She pretended!

Palae.   Go! Bring out the sword!

Scele.   I'll see that it's here immediately.
                        (*exit into the soldier's house*)

Palae.   (*to audience*) The infantry and the cavalry
    Are manned by men in their prime;
But for sheer pluck or derring-do,
    The girls win every time!   465
The way she managed both her roles:
    Didn't you find her clever?
She made that idiotic guard
    Look sillier than ever!
What fun to have a space to crawl
From house to house right through the wall!

48

(*Enter* SCELEDRUS, *stunned, from the soldier's house.*)

Scele.   Oh, Palaestrio, the sword's
Not necessary.

Palae.   What? Why not?

Scele.   She's there at home—master's girl.

Palae.   At home?

Scele.   She's lying on her couch.   470

Palae.   Holy Pollux, if this is true,
You've got yourself in a lovely mess.

Scele.   How's that?

Palae.   Because you dared to touch
That lady from the house next door.

Scele.   I feel sick.

Palae.   There can't be any
Other explanation:
That person is our girl's twin sister.
It was she that you saw kissing.

Scele.   Obviously she's the one,
Just as you say. I would have been   475
On the brink of death, if I'd spoken out.

Palae.   If you're wise, you'll keep it under your hat:
A slave may know, but mustn't tell.
I'm leaving now; I've no desire
To get mixed up with all your plans.
I'm going to visit my neighbor here;
Your meddling muddles make me tired.
If master comes and asks for me,
Look for me here; here's where I'll be.   480
                     (*exit into the old man's house*)

49

Act II, Scene 6

Scele.   So he's gone, has he? Couldn't care less for his master's
Business! Plays the part of a part-time slave!
Well, she's at home inside here now, for sure,
'Cause I just found her lying on her bed.
My mind's made up to be a watchdog now.   485

(*Enter* PERIPLECTOMENUS, *from his own house. He pretends to be unaware of* SCELEDRUS, *but speaks for his benefit.*)

Perip.   So help me Hercules, these slaves next door
Must think I've had a sudden change of sex:
They mock me like a woman! And my guest,
The girl who came from Athens yesterday,
To be tricked and treated like a common slut!   490

Scele.   Oh, help! He's heading headlong straight for me.
I'm afraid I may be in a mighty mess,
To judge from what I heard this old man say.

Perip.   (*aside*) I'll take him on. (*aloud*) Hey, numbskull Sceledrus,
Did you make fun of that girl who's staying with me?   495

Scele.   Dear neighbor, sir, please listen.

Perip.   Me listen to you?

Scele.   I want to clear myself.

Perip.   You clear yourself?
After doing a deed so wild and wicked?
Do you think your precious army connections
Give you the right to do what you want, jailbird?   500

Scele.   May I speak?

Perip.   So help me gods and goddesses,
I'm going to see you flogged and flayed alive,
Tormented all day long, from dawn to dusk.
You broke the tiles and gutters on my roof,
While you were trying to catch your monkey friend.   505

Next, you spied on my house and on my guest,
Who had his dear beloved in his arms;
You dared to charge your master's blameless girl
With foul behavior, me with infamy;
Abused my lady guest at my front door!   510
Unless I see you punished with the lash,
I'll cram that master of yours more full of shame
Than the sea is full of waves in a winter storm.

Scele.   I'm so confused, Periplectomenus, I don't know
Whether I ought to get annoyed with you . . .   515
But maybe your girl isn't ours and she's not her,
And then I ought to clear myself with you.
In fact, right now, I don't know what I saw:
That girl of yours is so much like our own,
If she isn't the same.

Perip.   Take a look inside; you'll see.   520

Scele.   You'd let me?

Perip.   No, I order you. Take your time.

Scele.   That's just what I'll do. (*exit into old man's house*)

Perip.   (*rushing to the door of the soldier's house*)
                 Quick, Philocomasium,
Battle stations! Run to my house on the run!
Later, when Sceledrus leaves my house, double quick
Make your run on the run back home again.   525
Ye gods, I'm sure she's bungled it.
If he doesn't see the girl—he's at the door.

Scele.   (*returning from the old man's house*)
Holy gods almighty! For heaven to make
Two different women more identical: 530
Impossible!

Perip.   Well?

Scele.   I've made a mess of things.

Perip.   Is she the one?

Scele.   She is, and yet she isn't.

Perip.   Did you see her?

Scele.   Yes, I saw her and your guest
Hugging and kissing.

Perip.   Is she the one?

Scele.   I don't know!

Perip.   Do you want to know for sure?

Scele.   Of course.

Perip.   Go inside   535
Your house at once; see if your girl's in there.

Scele.   Fine. That's good advice. I'll be right back.
                    (*exit into the soldier's house*)

Perip.   Great Pollux! I've never seen any man
Duped and doped in such a funny way!
Look: here he comes.

Scele.   (*returning from the soldier's house*)
                              Periplectomenus, I beg you   540
In the name of gods and men, by my lack of brains
And by your knees—

Perip.   To do what?

Scele.   To forgive
My ignorance and stupidity. Now at last
I know I was a blind and brainless idiot.
Philocomasium's there inside.

Perip.   What now,   545
Jailbird? Have you seen both girls?

Scele.	Yes, I have.	
Perip.	I want you to produce your master.	
Scele.	I've earned a dreadful drubbing, I confess, And I admit I wronged that guest of yours. But I thought she was master's concubine, The girl our soldier'd given me to guard. Two pails of water from a single well Aren't more alike than this girl and your guest. Yes, and I peeked through your skylight at you, I confess.	550
Perip.	You confess! I was a witness! And while my two young guests were kissing there, You saw them?	555
Scele.	I saw them. Why deny what I saw? But I thought I'd seen Philocomasium.	
Perip.	So! Did you think I was such a worthless man That I'd knowingly allow that girl to do Such horrible harm to my neighbor, in my house?	560
Scele.	Now, when I see the truth, I realize I acted foolishly; I meant no harm.	
Perip.	You meant no good! A slave should always keep His eyes and hands and tongue in firm control.	
Scele.	If I so much as mumble from now on, Even about a thing I know for sure, Then have me tortured: I'll submit to you. This time, forgive me, please.	565
Perip.	I'll try my best To think you meant no harm in this affair. I'll forgive you this time.	
Scele.	May the gods love you!	570

53

Perip. By Herc, if the gods love you, you'll hold your tongue;
Henceforth, you'll not know even what you know,
You'll not see what you've seen.

Scele.   Superb advice.
That's just my plan. Have I begged enough?

Perip.   Yes, go!

Scele. Nothing else I can do for you?

Perip.   Stay out of my life!   575

Scele. (*to himself, as he begins to leave*)
He's fooling me. How wonderfully kind and generous
Not to get angry! I know what he's doing:
As soon as the soldier comes back home from town,
I'll be arrested. He and Palaestrio
Are out to get me; I've known for quite a while.   580
They'll never lure me into that fishy trap;
I'll run away somewhere and hide for a couple of days,
Until this row dies down and tempers cool.
For I'm more damned than a whole damned city of sin.

Oh, hell! Come what may, I'll just go home.[6]   585
(*exit into the soldier's house*)

Perip. He's gone. I swear to Pollux, I'm quite sure
That any squealing pig has far more brains!
He's been deprived of seeing what he saw!
His eyes and ears and even his mind have fled
To our side. So far, things have gone just fine.   590
This woman's done a quite delightful job.

I'll go back to our senate; for Palaestrio's
At my house now, with Sceledrus away:
A full-scale senate meeting can be held.
I'll enter: mustn't miss the muster call.   595
(*exit into his own house*)

---

[6]Some editors have deleted this line, finding it inconsistent with what Sceledrus has just said
and with Periplectomenus' comment about Sceledrus in line 593. It does appear, however, that
Sceledrus is still at home in Act III, Scene 2. Plautus is often rather careless about such details.

ACT III

Enter PALAESTRIO *through Periplectomenus' door, stage right. As he emerges, he is talking over his shoulder to his fellow conspirators, who do not appear at once.*

Act III, Scene 1

Palae.   Keep back, you two, inside the doorway
(Just for a moment, Pleusicles),
Let me scout first to make sure
That there's no one here to spy on us
When we hold our secret council.
Our need now is for safe ground
Where no enemy can attack
And plunder this wonderful plan of ours.

(*to audience*)
A well-planned scheme looks badly planned
If your enemies can use it,   600
And if your enemies can use it,
It never fails to ruin you.
You see, however well contrived,
A plan is often snatched away
If you're not careful to take some thought
In choosing the place to hatch the plot.
In fact, if sómehow your enemies
Come to learn your clever scheme,
They'll put that scheme of yours to work:
They'll tie your tongue and bind your hands   605
And in the end they'll do to you
What you had meant to do to them.

I'll check on the left side and the right,
Then look all round to make quite sure
That there's no hunter lying low

55

> To fold his ears around our plan.
> From here the outlook's beautifully barren,
> All the way to the end of the street.
> I'll call them. Periplectomenus!
> Hey, Pleusicles! Come on outside.   610

(*Enter* PERIPLECTOMENUS *and* PLEUSICLES. *Palaestrio's original master is an attractive and well-mannered young man, but not very quick on the uptake.*)

Perip.   Here we are, at your command.

Palae.   It's easy to command good men like you.
What I want to know is this: do we use
The same plan we thought up inside?

Perip.   It seems perfect for our needs.

Palae.   What do you say, Pleusicles?

Pleus.   If you two like it, would I object?
Could I get a better friend than you?

Palae.   There's a polite and pleasant statement!   615

Perip.   A very appropriate thing to say!

Pleus.   But there's one circumstance that racks
My heart with agonizing pain.

Perip.   What circumstance is that? Speak out!

Pleus.   That I should trouble a man like you
(At your age!) with this childishness!
It's beneath your virtue and dignity.
You're using all your energy
In working for my selfish ends;   620
Assisting in my love affair!
And all the while you're doing things
That men of your age, as a rule,

Would sooner shun than undertake.
I'm so ashamed to be causing you
So much distress in your old age.

Palae. As lovers go, you're very strange
If you feel shame for what you've done.
You can't be a lover, Pleusicles;
You're the shadow of a man in love!   625

Pleus. Does being a lover make it right
For me to bother this old man?

Perip. What do you mean? Do you really think
That I've got both feet in the grave?
Am I fit for the coffin? Do I appear
To have spent so many years on earth?
As a matter of fact, my age right now
Is a hale and hearty fifty-four:
My eyesight's fine; I'm not so fragile;
My feet are quick; my hands are agile.   630

Palae. His hair is white as white can be:
But old at heart? No sir, not he!
Since birth, he's lived in prime condition,
Blessed with a tranquil disposition.

Pleus. Honest to Pollux, I've seen that;
You are quite right, Palaestrio.
When it comes to kindness, this man here
Is every bit as young as I.

Perip. Yes, my friend, the more you test me,
All the more you'll come to know   635
My friendliness toward your love.

Pleus. Why test you when I know it now?

Perip. Reliable experience
Is never gained at second hand.
Unless you've been in love yourself,
You'll scarcely read a lover's heart.

I too have sparks of love still glowing,
All my juices still are flowing,   640
I'm not quite as dry as dust—
I've had a pleasant life of lust.

I can be witty, gay, and bright,
Or play the tactful guest all night,
Whichever you want. I'm never the galling
Type who contradicts a host:
Tactless manners I find appalling;
Tact and taste are uppermost.
I always deliver, with fine elocution,
My conversational contribution.   645
Likewise, I know how to keep quiet
When it's another man's turn to try it.
You'll never see me spit or cough
Or fail to blow my nose—not me!
After all, I was born in Ephesus,
Not in southern Italy!

Palae.   What a delightfully young old man,
            If he's as good as he says he is.
            It's obvious, he was raised as a child
            In the tender care of the Goddess of Charm.   650

Perip.   I'll prove what a charming man I am;
            You'll see—I'll be better than my word.

            At banquets, I am never found
            Seducing someone else's girl,
            Or grabbing choicest chunks of meat,
            Or gulping down a glass of wine.
            When partying, I'm never first
            To start a drunken argument:
            If anyone's annoying me,
            I shut my mouth and head for home.   655
            Whenever I'm dining I'm always a shining
            Example of love and loveliness.

Palae.   Heavenly Pollux! Your character
            Is simply blossoming with charm!

I'd be willing to pay their weight in gold
To get three men as good as you.

Pleus.   I can tell you, you won't find
Another man at his ripe age
Who's more urbane in all respects
Or friendlier to every friend.   660

Perip.   I'll make you admit that I'm still young
When it comes to personality:
Whatever you're doing, I'll show up
Teeming with little favors for you.

Do you need a witness in court
Who's stern and angry? Look, it's me!
A gentle one, maybe? You'll say that I
Am gentler far than the ocean calm,
Than I'm more limpid and liquid smooth
Than the caress of the western breeze.   665
To suit your needs, I can make myself
An entertaining dinner guest,
Or a practically perfect parasite,
Or a butler—the best in the business.
As for dancing, no prancing fairy
Has steps as neat and sweet as mine.

Palae.   (*to* PLEUS.) What do you think you'd choose to crown
These talents, if you had the choice?

Pleus.   I'd like to be able to show him all
The gratitude he's earned from me.   670
You've earned it, too; I'm well aware
What a terrible nuisance I am to you.
But for me to cause you such expense—
It hurts me.

Perip.   You're an idiot.
What a man spends on a bad wife
Or on an enemy—that's real expense;
On a good guest and on a friend
Money spent is money saved;

And whatever is spent on the gods' account
The wise man reckons as capital gain.   675
It's thanks to the gods I've got the means
To be such a generous host to you;
Eat and drink, relax yourself,
Get loaded with laughter along with me.
My house is a free one, I'm a free one,
Too: I like to live for myself.
With all my wealth and influence
(Thank heaven for it, I may say)
I could have found a wife with a dowry,
Married a girl from the upper crust;   680
But I don't want to have a spouse
Who'll yap and bitch around the house.

Palae.   Come now! To have a little son
And to be a father: that's nice.

Perip.   Ye gods! To have a little fun
And be free from bother: much nicer.

Palae.   Sir, you have that rare ability
To guide yourself and your fellow man!

Perip.   Now, a good wife's a thing of joy,
If there's any place on the face of the earth   685
Where such a creature can be found;
But I know that the sort of bride I'd get
Would never be likely to say to me:

    "Please, dear husband, buy me some wool,
    And I'll knit you a sweater that's soft and warm;
    I'll make you a lovely overcoat
    So you won't shiver when winter comes."

(You'd never hear that from any wife!)
If I had a wife, her voice would wake me
At dawn, before the cocks were crowing: 690

    "Please, dear husband, give me some money,
    Mother needs a little present.

Give me some cash to buy some candy;
Give me some money to give next Sunday
To the sorceress, the dream-diviner,
The psychic, and the entrail-gazer;
If I don't have cash, I'll enrage the lady
Who tells the future from my eyebrows.
There's no diplomatic way
Of avoiding a gift for the laundry maid;   695
For days on end, the girl in the pantry
Has fumed because she's had no tip.
The midwife, too, is extremely cross
Because I've been ungenerous.
Aren't you going to give anything
To the nurse who looks after the little slaves?"

All these feminine expenses
(And you can be sure of many others)
Keep me from wanting to wed a wife
Who'd always be weaving words like these.   700

Palae.   I hope the gods are on your side!
          Great Herc! If ever you expel
          That freedom of yours, you'll find it hard
          To get it safely reinstated!

Pleus.   But it's a guarantee of fame
          In a great and wealthy family
          To bring up children; they provide
          A living self-memorial.

Perip.   When I've got so many relatives
          Why in the world should I need children?   705
          As it is, I'm a happy man,
          And I live my life the way I want.
          I'll give all I've got to my relatives
          When I die: I'll divide it among them all.
          Meanwhile, they'll flock to me, constantly talk to me,
          Watch what I'm doing, ask what I want.
          Long before dawn they'll all be here
          Wanting to know how I slept last night.
          Those who send me lovely gifts

Will substitute for real sons.   710
When they roast a sacrificial calf
My share is bigger than their own.
They drag me to the feast! They're always
Inviting me to lunch or dinner;
The one who serves me the poorest supper
Feels most miserable of men.
My relatives are rivals with their gifts,
And me—I murmur quietly:
    "Though it's my money they're gaping at,
    It's me they're making rich and fat."   715

Palae. What insight's here! What foresight clear!
How well you furnish the needs of life!
You're so well off, it's just like having
Twins or triplets in the house!

Perip. Holy Pollux, if I'd had a real son,
I'd have had an endless supply of trouble.
I'd feel continual mental anguish:
If he was sick in bed with a fever   720
I'd think he was dying; if he fell down
Drunk or tumbled from a horse,
I'd become a nervous wreck,
Afraid he'd broken his leg or neck.

Pleus. This man deserves enormous wealth
And the longest life the gods can give:
He guards what he has, he enjoys himself,
And he's most obliging to his friends.

Palae. A delightful personality!
So help me heaven, if heaven were fair   725
The gods would not have been content
With one design for all our lives.
Compare how merchandise is priced
By an honest government inspector:
When the stuff is decent, he sets a price
That will get it sold for its proper worth;
When the stuff is poor, he fines the owner
The full face value of the goods!

Well, honest gods would have divided
Human life on a similar scheme: 730
To a man of delightful personality
They'd give a long and lasting life;
But those who were wicked and criminal
Would die a swift and speedy death.

If the gods had followed this simple plan,
(a) There'd be far fewer bad men around;
(b) When they did commit crimes, they'd act
With far less swagger, and finally,
(c) For all the honest types
The cost of living would come down!   735

Perip.   To find fault with the plans of the gods
Is foolish and ignorant; it is
The equivalent of blasphemy.
You'd better stop that kind of talk.

Now I want to buy provisions,
My guest, to welcome you into my house
As you deserve and as I desire:
With good face, with good grace, and with good food.

Pleus.   Please, I'm certainly not unhappy
At what you've spent on me so far.   740
No one can possibly hope to have
A friend so warm and generous
That he can stay for three whole days
Without becoming a bit of a pain;
But when he's stayed ten days on end,
Well, that's a downright siege of Troy!
Even if the host is holding out
Without bad grace, the slaves will grumble.

Perip.   I've taken steps to guarantee
My slaves all slave away for me;   745
They're not inclined to boss me around,
My friend; you won't see me kowtow.
If they're upset at what I want,
I steer the ship and crack the whip;

If they hate a job they've got to do it
Willy-nilly, like it or not.
Now I'm off to do the shopping
I said I'd do.

Pleus.   If your mind's made up,
Shop moderately—no great expense:
Anything at all's enough for me.   750

Perip.   Come on, come off it, take away
That old and rusty platitude.
My dear young friend, you mustn't repeat
The tired clichés of the men in the street.
You'll hear them say, when they come to dinner,
When the main course has been served:
  "Why did you go to all this trouble?
  Such extravagance just for me?
  Holy Herc, you must be crazy,
  This would be enough for ten!"   755
Whatever food you've bought for them,
They groan and frown—and gulp it down.

Palae.   That's exactly how it happens.
What a shrewd and keen intelligence!

Perip.   But these same people never say,
However high the table's piled:
  "Have that removed; take out this dish;
  Oh, no ham, please, I don't care for it;
  Away with that juicy slice of pork;
  This lovely eel will be better cold,   760
  Off, out, away!"
                  You'd never hear
These pronouncements from any of them;
No, they hurl themselves onto the table,
Feet off the ground, as they glut themselves.

Palae.   A good description of bad manners!

Perip.   I haven't delivered a hundredth part
Of the total lecture I could give,
If only we had sufficient time.

Palae.	Yes. Well, then, the matter at hand:
	This should be our first concern. 765
	Now please pay attention, both of you.
	I need your help, Periplectomenus.
	I've thought up a delicious little trick
	To get our soldier clipped and shorn
	Of all his lovely locks—and give
	Our Philocomasium's lover here
	An ideal opportunity
	To spirit her away and keep her.
Perip.	I'd love to share that plan of yours. 770
Palae.	Well I would love to share that ring
	Of yours.
Perip.	What in the world for?
Palae.	When I've got it, then I'll give
	A full account of my little scheme.
Perip.	Use it, take it!
Palae.	Take from me
	In return the trick that I've devised.
Perip.	We're both listening, ears wide open.
Palae.	My master likes to play around with women,
	More, I believe, than any man 775
	Who ever was or ever will be.
Perip.	I share that belief myself.
Palae.	He says, moreover, he's *so* handsome—
	Far better looking than Alexander.
	All the women in Ephesus
	Are chasing him—or so he claims.
Perip.	Holy Pollux, many husbands
	Wish that claim were really true!
	But I know perfectly well that he's

This way. Get on, Palaestrio,   780
Weigh me a few of your shortest words
And wrap them up as fast as you can.

Palae. All right. Can you find me a woman,
          Absolutely beautiful,
          Well stacked and well stocked
          With a sense of fun and trickery?

Perip. Freeborn or the daughter of a slave?

Palae. I couldn't care less, provided
          You get me a professional,
          The type that's always self-employed;   785
          She must have a clever breast (I can't
          Say "brain": no woman has one of those!)

Perip. Do you want her green, or fully ripened?

Palae. Just like this: luscious, juicy,
          The most delicious you can find,
          And young—oh, young, especially.

Perip. I've got the girl: a client of mine,
          Who's young, eye-filling, and bed-willing.
          But what use will we make of her?

Palae. You'll conduct her now to your house;   790
          Then you'll bring her here dressed up
          In the fashion of a noble matron
          (You know: hair swept up and bound
          In a roll), and have her pretend that she's
          Your wife. She must be taught this story.

Pleus. I seem to have lost your train of thought.

Palae. You'll find it again. (*to* PERIP.) But has she a maid,
          Perhaps?

Perip.   Yes, and sharp as a tack.

Palae. We need her too. You must tell this story

	To the woman and her little maid:	795
	She's to pretend that she's your wife	

	To the woman and her little maid:	795
	She's to pretend that she's your wife	
	And dying of love for our soldier here;	
	That she gave this ring to her loyal slave,	
	The maid, who gave it next to me,	
	As a kind of middleman, to pass	
	Along to the soldier.	

Perip.   I hear you.
Please don't pound me until I'm deaf;
My ears are really very good.

Palae.   I'll give it to him, saying it's
Been offered to me by your wife,   800
To win him over to her cause.
The way he is, he'll fall, poor sap:
His dirty mind is never set
On anything but adultery.

Perip.   If you gave the job to the sun in the sky
To search for girls, he couldn't find
Two lovelier women for this job
Than I have. Keep your spirits up!

Palae.   All right, look after it, but be quick!
                      (*exit* PERIPLECTOMENUS)
Now listen to me, Pleusicles.   805

Pleus.   Your obedient servant, sir.

Palae.   Do this:
When the soldier reaches the house,
Remember not to call Philocomasium
By her right name.

Pleus.   What name shall I use?

Palae.   Justine.

Pleus.   Of course. The very name
We chose before.

Palae.	Enough! Please go.

Pleus.   I'll remember. But why it matters
To remember, I'd still like to know.

Palae.   I'll tell you at the moment when
The need demands. Meanwhile, keep quiet!   810
(*nodding after* PERIPLECTOMENUS)
Exactly as he's acting now,
Play your part actively as well.

Pleus.   I'm going inside, then. (*exit into old man's house*)

Palae.   Only try
To keep your head and follow orders.

Act III, Scene 2

Palae.   What a commotion! What a mighty plan!
Today I'll kidnap the soldier's concubine,
If the men in the ranks keep battle discipline.   815
I'll call my friend. Hey, Sceledrus, if you're not too busy,
Step outside the house. Palaestrio wants you.

(LURCIO, *a drunken slave, enters staggering from the soldier's house.*)

Lurcio   Sceledrus 'sbusy.

Palae.   How?

Lurcio   He's asleep and snorting.

Palae.   What do you mean, "snorting"?

Lurcio   I meant to say "snoring."
But somehow 'sall the same, you snore, you snort—   820

Palae.   Ah! Is Sceledrus sleeping inside?

Lurcio   Not his nose:

68

It's roaring away. He snitched a cup on the sly . . .
Back in the cellar . . . spicing the jars . . . wine-steward.

Palae. Haha. You crook! All right, assistant steward—   825

Lurcio What do you want?

Palae.   How did he manage to fall asleep?

Lurcio With his eyes, I guess.

Palae.   That's not my question, stupid!
Go on. You're done for unless I hear the truth.
Did you pour out wine for him?

Lurcio   No.

Palae.   You deny it?

Lurcio Of course I deny it; he ordered me not to speak.   830
I didn't pour out eight half-pints into a jug
And he didn't drink it hot for his lunch, either.

Palae. And you didn't drink?

Lurcio   I'll be damned if I drank!
I couldn't drink!

Palae.   Why not?

Lurcio   I had to gulp it down.
It was so hot, my throat was getting burned.   835

Palae. *They* get tight and *we* drink vinegar-water!
What a pair of cellar bottle-openers!

Lurcio You'd do the same, if you had charge of the cellar.
You're jealous because you can't keep up to us.   840

Palae. Hey! Did he ever open wine before?
Answer me, you good-for-nothing!

And to help you remember, I'll tell you this:
If you lie, Lurcio, you'll get crucified!

Lurcio   Oh yeah? You want to give public evidence.
And when I'm fired from my cellar sinecure,   845
You and some friend will wangle the wine detail.

Palae.   Holy Pollux, no! Buck up, speak out!

Lurcio   I swear I never saw him pour it. It was this way:
He'd give the word, then I'd pour out the wine.

Palae.   That's why those jars were standing on their heads!   850

Lurcio   No! This is why the jars were tipping over:
In the cellar there were little slippery spots,
And a two-quart jug was close to the jars (like this)
And it got filled up ten times! I saw it
Filling up and getting empty. The jug kept rolling   855
On the floor in ecstasy, and the jars kept tipping.

Palae.   Go on, get inside! While you play holy roller
In the cellar, I'll get master from the forum.

Lurcio   (*aside*) I'm through! He'll torture me if he comes home
And hears about all this from someone else.
I'll run away somewhere and postpone my fate.   860
(*to audience*) Don't tell this fellow, please, word of honor!

Palae.   Where are *you* going?

Lurcio   I'm on an errand; I'll be back soon.

Palae.   Who sent you?

Lurcio   Philocomasium.

Palae.   Well, hurry back!

Lurcio   By the way, if he's handing out punishments   865
When I'm not around, I'd like you to have my share.

                                      (*exit*)

Palae. I've just realized what the girl has done:
Sceledrus fell asleep, so she sent away
This other guard, to have a chance to cross over. Good!

Here's Periplectomenus with the woman I asked him   870
To bring. She's gorgeous! The gods are helping us.
What dignity and class! Not at all like a courtesan!
This business is starting to shape up beautifully.

Act III, Scene 3

Enter PERIPLECTOMENUS *with the two women that he has promised to bring, the
luscious courtesan* ACROTELEUTIUM *and her maid* MILPHIDIPPA. PALAESTRIO
stands to one side and watches unobserved.

Perip. I've told you, Acroteleutium,
And you too, Milphidippa;
I explained the plan at your house.
If you have the slightest doubt about   875
This flimflam and skulduggery,
I'd like you to hear it all again;
But if you understand it, we've
Got better things to chat about.

Acrot. My dearest patron, I would look
A fool—an utter idiot—
If I took on a job for someone,
Promising to give my all,
And then when I was on the job
I couldn't be both loose and sly.   880

Perip. It's always best to have advice.

Acrot. Advice? A professional like me?
That's hardly needed, heaven knows!
Didn't I tell you, on my own,
After my ears were merely washed
By the first wave of your appeal,
Just how the soldier should be trimmed?

Perip. No one alone can know it all.

71

	I've seen a lot of people sail	885
	Right past the land of good advice
	And never set foot on the shore.

Acrot. If a woman has to do a job
That's wicked and malicious,
She needs no reminder or advice—
Her memory's eternal;
But if she must take on a task
That's good or honest, suddenly
She's troubled by forgetfulness
And can't remember anything!   890

Perip. That's why I'm frightened. You've a job
To do that's good and wicked both:
When you two work your worst upon
The soldier, that will help my cause.

Acrot. Just as long as we don't know
We're doing a good deed, have no fear.

Perip. You do deserve some dire disaster!

Acrot. Hey! Don't worry, we can take it.   895

Perip. That's the spirit! Follow me.

Palae. (*aside*) Why should I wait to go and meet them?
(*to* PERIPLECTOMENUS) I'm so glad to see you back,
With the lovely equipment you've got there.

Perip. Ah, you've come at the right moment,
Palaestrio. Look! Here they are,
The girls you asked me to bring along,
All dressed up.

Palae.   Hurrah! My friend for life!
I'm Palaestrio, Acroteleutium.

Acrot. Who is he, I'd like to know?   900
He uses my name like an old friend.

72

Perip.   This man's our master craftsman.

Acrot.   Hi, master craftsman.

Palae.   Hi, yourself.
Tell me, has he loaded you
With your instructions?

Perip.   These two girls
Have both been perfectly rehearsed.

Palae.   I want to hear exactly how;
I'm scared you may have made a slip.

Perip.   I've now transmitted your instructions,
Adding nothing of my own.   905

Acrot.   Do you really want your boss, the soldier,
Made a laughingstock?

Palae.   You said it!

Acrot.   All is delightfully, ever so cleverly,
Beautifully, dutifully ready.

Palae.   I want you to pretend that you're
The wife of this man here.

Acrot.   So be it.

Palae.   Making believe you're head over heels
In love with the soldier.

Acrot.   You'll see it done!

Palae.   And that this affair is being arranged
By your maid, with me as middleman.   910

Acrot.   You could have been a professional prophet:
You tell the future perfectly.

Palae.   And that your lovely little maid
Has brought this ring along to me,
So I can give it to the soldier
With your message.

Acrot.   Right again!

Perip.   What's the point of dismembering
Their memorized plans?

Acrot.   It's a good idea.
Dearest patron, you must realize
That when there's a proper master craftsman,   915
Once he gets the keel of a boat
Lined up absolutely straight,
It's easy to build the rest of the ship
On his firmly laid foundation.
Now this keel's been truly laid,
Carpenters are all at hand,
And a foreman, skilled in supervision.
If we're not kept waiting by the man
Who's supplying the raw material,   920
From what I know of our enterprise
And skill, the ship will soon be launched.

Palae.   I suppose you know my master, the soldier?

Acrot.   What a silly question!
How could I help but know that
Widely dreaded, curly-headed,
Loud-speaking, perfume-reeking lecher?

Palae.   And he doesn't know you?

Acrot.   He's never seen me:
How should he know who I am?

Palae.   Oh, what a lovely piece of news!   925
Our game will be lovelier than ever.

Acrot.   Can't you simply hand me the man

74

And then keep quiet and relax?
If I fail to trick him marvellously,
Please lay all the blame on me.

Palae.   Come on then, go along inside,
Get after this business with all your wits.

Acrot.   O.K. Your worries are over.

Palae.   Periplectomenus, take these girls
Inside for now. I'm off to the forum   930
To find him and present this ring;
I'll tell him that your wife gave it to me
And that she's dying with love for him.
I want you two to send this girl
To us, as soon as we come back.
She'll play the secret messenger.

Perip.   We'll do it, don't you worry.

Palae.   Attend to your job; I'll bring him here
Loaded, primed, and ready to go. (*exit stage left*)   935

Perip.   Have a good walk, do a good job!
(*to* ACROTELEUTIUM) If I can work out all the details
Of this affair, so that today
My guest can have the soldier's mistress
And take her away from here to Athens—
If only we can trip this trap,
Oh, what a gift you'll get from me!

Acrot.   Is the girl providing help herself?   940

Perip.   Charmingly and disarmingly.

Acrot.   The future's well assured, I know.
When our wicked talents have been combined,
Never fear, we'll be triumphant
Through underhanded treachery.

Perip.   Well, then, we should go inside

To think this through with cool minds,
And carefully and properly
Rehearse the job we've got to do,   945
So, when the soldier comes, there'll be
No slip-up.

Acrot.   Let's get going, then!
(*The two* WOMEN *accompany* PERIPLECTOMENUS *into his house.*)

ACT IV

Enter PYRGOPOLYNICES *from the forum* (*stage left*), *accompanied by* PALAES-
TRIO *and other* SLAVES.

Act IV, Scene 1

Pyrgo.   What a joy, when you're doing a job,
And it turns out nicely, the way you want!
Today I sent my parasite
On a trip to visit King Seleucus,
So that Seleucus could be shown
The fine recruits I signed up here:
Enough to keep his kingdom safe
And let me take a little rest.   950

Palae.   Why not look after your own affairs
And forget Seleucus? I've got something
New and dazzling arranged for you!
I am acting as middleman.

Pyrgo.   All other matters will have to wait:
I give you my absolute attention.
(*He dismisses the other* SLAVES.)
Speak: I now surrender my ears
Into your sole authority.

Palae.   Look around: we don't want a spy
To pounce on our conversation.   955
This affair was entrusted to me
To be handled with utter secrecy.

Pyrgo.   There's no one here.

77

Palae.   This little token
          Of love—first, take it from me.

Pyrgo.   What's this? Where's it from?

Palae.   It comes
          From a dazzling lady who's fond of fun;
          She loves you and is lusting for
          Your pure and perfect pulchritude.
          It's her ring. Just now her maid
          Gave it to me to bring to you.   960

Pyrgo.   What's her status? Freeborn or only
          A wave of the wand away from slavery?

Palae.   Come on! Would I dare to speak to you
          As a go-between from a former slave,
          You, who can never find the time
          For the freeborn girls who are after you?

Pyrgo.   Is she married or unattached?

Palae.   She's married
          And unattached.

Pyrgo.   How can she be   965
          At the same time married and unattached?

Palae.   She's a young bride with an old husband.

Pyrgo.   Hurray!

Palae.   She's lovely, luscious, and
          Refined!

Pyrgo.   Be careful to tell the truth!

Palae.   Her beauty's almost a match for yours.

Pyrgo.   Holy Herc, she must be gorgeous!
          But who is she?

Palae.	The wife of Periplectomenus,

Palae.   The wife of Periplectomenus,
This old gentleman next door.
She's dying for you and dearly wants
To leave him: she detests the fellow.   970
Now she's ordered me to beg
And implore you to give her the power
And the opportunity to do it.

Pyrgo.   Sweet Hercules, I want it if she does!

Palae.   She? *Want* it?

Pyrgo.   But what shall we do
With that concubine who's in the house?

Palae.   Why not tell her to go away
Wherever she wants? In fact, her mother
And twin sister have just arrived
Here in Ephesus, looking for her.   975

Pyrgo.   *What?* Here in Ephesus, her mother?

Palae.   I've got it on good authority.

Pyrgo.   Holy Herc, what a lovely chance
To kick that woman out of the house!

Palae.   Wait! Would you like to do the job
In a lovely way?

Pyrgo.   Speak. What's your plan?

Palae.   Do you want to remove her double quick,
And have her leave without bad will?

Pyrgo.   Yes.

Palae.   Then this is what you should do.
You've absolutely loads of money;   980
Tell the girl to keep as gifts
The gold and trinkets you've piled on her.

Tell her to leave you and go away,
Taking them wherever she wants.

Pyrgo. Good advice; but be careful to see
That I don't lose her and then have this girl
Change her mind.

Palae.   Hah! You're a fine one!
She loves you as if you were her own eyes.

Pyrgo. It's Venus who loves me.

Palae.   Shh! Be quiet!
The door's opening. Come here quietly.   985
That little cruiser coming this way
Is the woman's go-between.

Pyrgo. What little cruiser?

Palae.   Her maid,
Who's coming out of the house this way.
She brought me that ring I gave you.

Pyrgo. Holy Pollux, she's not bad
Herself!

Palae.   Compared to the other girl
She's like a crow or a chimpanzee.
Look at her eyes! She's on the track;
She's listening, waiting to attack.   990

Act IV, Scene 2

MILPHIDIPPA, *who has been visible for some time, speaks first to the audience.*

Milph. In front of the house is the arena
Where now I must hold my little circus.
I'll pretend that I don't see them
Or even know that they're about.

Pyrgo.	Quiet, let's be eavesdroppers To hear if she mentions me at all.
Milph.	(*in a loud "soliloquy"*) I hope there's no one near who meddles In matters that aren't his own concern, Someone who'd spy on what I'm doing, Some loafer from the idle rich. They're the people I'm afraid of: They'd be a nuisance or get in the way, If they're out here while she's in there. She wants this fellow desperately, My poor, unhappy mistress. And now Her heart is all aflutter for him, That simply lovely, simply gorgeous Soldier, Pyrgopolynices.
Pyrgo.	Has *she* fallen for me as well? She's praising my looks. Holy Pollux, Her conversation needs no wax!
Palae.	How so?
Pyrgo.	Because she speaks With shining polish and spotless elegance.
Palae.	She's got *you* to talk about: A shining topic of conversation!
Pyrgo.	Well, she herself is a simply Lovely, simply sparkling girl. Holy Hercules, she's starting To please me a little, Palaestrio.
Palae.	Before you've even seen the other?
Pyrgo.	I can take the other on faith. Besides, she's absent, and this little cruiser Is forcing me to love her.

995

1000

1005

81

Palae.   Great Herc,
                 Don't fall for her; she's engaged to me!
                 If the other girl marries you today,
                 This one will become my wife.

Pyrgo.   Then why do you wait to talk to her?

Palae.   All right, follow me.

Pyrgo.   Your humble servant.

Milph.   (*continuing her "soliloquy"*)
                 How I wish I could have a chance
                 To meet the gentleman on whose
                 Account I've come outside the house.   1010

Palae.   (*aloud*) That wish of yours will soon come true;
                 Keep up your spirits, have no fear.
                 There's a certain man who knows where to find
                 What you want.

Milph.   Who was that I heard?

Palae.   A partner who shares and bears your plans.

Milph.   Oh, my! Then my secret isn't a secret.

Palae.   I'd say it's both secret and un-secret.

Milph.   How so?

Palae.   You keep secrets from those you don't trust:
                 I am your loyal, trusty friend.   1015

Milph.   Pass me the password, brother in Bacchus!

Palae.   "A certain woman loves a certain man."

Milph.   That's true of many girls.

Palae.	But not So many send a gift from their finger.
Milph.	Ah, I recognize you now, You've got me back on level ground. Is the man not here?
Palae.	Maybe yes, maybe no.
Milph.	Let me have you all alone.
Palae.	A short conversation or a long one?
Milph.	A word or two.
Palae.	(*to* Pyrgopolynices) I'll be back in a moment.
Pyrgo.	What of me? Shall I stand here all the while, A handsome hero going to waste?
Palae.	Stand there and stand it; I'm working for you.
Pyrgo.	Hurry up! Waiting tortures me.
Palae.	Easy does it—you know that!— It's the rule for this kind of merchandise.
Pyrgo.	All right, have it your own sweet way.
Palae.	(*aside*) I've never seen a stone so stupid. (*to* Milphidippa, *sotto voce*) Here I am again. What did you want me for?
Milph.	To have a little conference On how you want this Troy to be sacked.
Palae.	Say she's crazy for him—
Milph.	I've got that.

1020

1025

Palae.	Praise his face, praise his physique,
	And mention his heroic deeds.

Milph.	I'm all sharpened for that job;
	I showed you just a moment ago.

Palae.	Then keep your wits and look around:
	Follow the trail and track my words.

Pyrgo.	Could you give me some small share of your
	Attention today?

At last! Here you are.   1030

Palae.	Yours to command.

Pyrgo.	What has she told you?

Palae.	She says her mistress is suffering torture,
	Wailing, weeping, all worn out,
	Because she wants you, because she needs you.
	This is why she's been sent to you.

Pyrgo.	Have her approach.

Palae.	You know what to do,
	I hope. Fill yourself with scorn
	And act displeased; criticize
	My offering you for mass consumption. 1035

Pyrgo.	I remember. I'll follow instructions.

Palae.	(*aloud*) Am I to summon the woman who wants you?

Pyrgo.	Have her approach and state her wish.

Palae.	Woman, approach, state your wish.

Milph.	Hello, handsome.

Pyrgo.	She actually knows my middle name!
	May the gods grant you all you ask.

Milph.   To spend a lifetime alone with you—

Pyrgo.   That's asking too much!

Milph.   Not me, silly,
But my mistress who's dying for you.

Pyrgo.   Many other women share that desire.   1040
Demand exceeds supply.

Milph.   Holy Castor,
No wonder you value yourself so highly!
You're so handsome, so distinguished
In accomplishments and manly beauty.
Was there ever a human who more deserved
To be a god?

Palae.   By God, he's not really
Human. (*aside to* MILPH.) I think a vulture has more
Humanity.

Pyrgo.   (*aside to* PALAESTRIO) I'll preen myself now,
Seeing that she's so high in my praise.

Palae.   (*to* MILPH.) Do you see how this no-good carries on?   1045
(*to* PYRGO.) Why not answer this woman? She's come
From the girl I mentioned a while ago.

Pyrgo.   Which one you mentioned? So many girls
Run after me, I can't remember them.

Milph.   From the woman who robs her fingers
And gives your fingers something to wear.
I took this ring from one who desires you.
Brought it to him; he gave it to you.

Pyrgo.   What do you want now, woman? Speak!

Milph.   She wants you so much: don't reject her.   1050
Her very life depends on you.
Her hope and despair are in your hands.

85

Pyrgo.   What does she want?

Milph.   To whisper in your ear,
To melt in your arms, to seethe in your embrace.
Unless you're willing to help her now,
She'll soon be pushed to utter despair.
Come, dear Achilles, say you'll do it,
In fairness save that lady fair;
Show your kind and generous nature,
Sacker of cities, slayer of kings!   1055

Pyrgo.   Holy Herc, what a nuisance!
How often have I told you, you good-for-nothing,
Not to keep promising my charms
To all and sundry?

Palae.   Do you hear that, woman?
I told you once and I'm telling you again:
If this wild boar isn't brought a gift
He's not likely to act as stud
For every pretty passing piglet.   1060

Milph.   He'll get whatever price he asks.

Palae.   He'll need three thousand golden drachmas:
His absolute rock-bottom price.

Milph.   Merciful Castor, that's too cheap!

Pyrgo.   I've never been a greedy man.
I've quite a bit of wealth already:
Over a thousand bushels of golden drachmas.

Palae.   Not counting his cash reserves! And his silver:
Not merely masses, but mountains of it!
Mount Etna isn't half as high.   1065

Milph.   (*aside to* PALAE.) Sweet Castor, what an awful liar!

Palae.   How am I doing?

Milph.	What about me? Am I spreading it on?
Palae.	You know what you're doing.
Milph.	(*to* PYRGO.) Please send me to get her right away.
Palae.	Can't you give her some reply? Say you either will or won't.
Milph.	Why torment that heartsick girl? She's never done you any harm.
Pyrgo.	Tell her to come out here to us. Say I'll do everything she wants.
Milph.	Now you're acting the way you should, 1070 When you go for a woman who goes for you—
Palae.	(*aside*) This girl was born with a sense of fun!
Milph.	—When you don't heap scorn upon my plea, When you treat my entreaty so generously. (*aside to* PALAE.) How's that? Am I doing well?
Palae.	Holy Herc, I can't stop laughing!
Milph.	That's why I had to hide my face!
Pyrgo.	By Pollux, woman, I hope you know What a great honor I'm doing her.
Milph.	I know it and I'll tell her that. 1075
Palae.	To another woman he could have sold This favor for money.
Milph.	I believe you.
Palae.	Perfect warriors are produced

> From women that he's made pregnant;
> Every child lives eight hundred years!

Milph. Come on, you're making fun of me!

Pyrgo. Actually, they live a thousand years,
From millennium to millennium.

Palae. (*to* PYRGOPOLYNICES) I cut the total down a bit
In case she thought I was lying to her.   1080

Milph. I'm staggered! How many years will he live
Himself, if his sons all live so long?

Pyrgo. My dear woman, I was born
Just one day after Jupiter.

Palae. If his birthday had been the day before,
This man would hold royal sway in heaven!

Milph. Please, please, enough! If I can,
Let me get away from you alive!

Palae. Then why not go, since you've got your answer?

Milph. I'll go and bring her here—the woman   1085
I'm acting for. Anything else you want?

Pyrgo. To be no more handsome than I am:
My beauty takes up so much time!

Palae. Are you still here? Be off!

Milph.   I'm gone.

Palae. One more thing—do you hear? Speak to her
With skill and art; thrill her heart—
(*aside*) Tell Philocomasium, if she's there,
To cross home; let her know he's here.

Milph. She's here with my mistress; both of them
Have secretly overheard our talk.   1090

Palae. Wonderful! If they've heard us talk
They'll be able to steer a perfect course.

Milph. (*as if outraged*) Out of my way, I'm leaving.

Palae. I'm not in your way, I'm not touching you,
I'm not—saying another word.

Pyrgo. Tell her to hurry and come out here.
We'll give her top priority.
                    (*exit* MILPHIDIPPA *into the old man's house*)

Act IV, Scene 3

Pyrgo. What's your advice to me now, Palaestrio,
About my concubine? I certainly can't   1095
Bring this one into the house before she goes.

Palae. Why ask me what to do? I've already told you
How to manage it most mercifully.
Let her have the gold and all the fancy clothes
You've lavished on her—keep them, pack them off.   1100
Tell her it's really high time she went home:
Her mother and twin sister have arrived;
She ought to head back in their company.

Pyrgo. How do you know they're here?

Palae.   With my own eyes
I saw her sister here.

Pyrgo.   Did they meet each other?   1105

Palae. Yes.

Pyrgo.   Did her sister seem . . . well built?

Palae. You want
Everything!

Pyrgo. Where's their mother? Did her sister say?

Palae. On the ship, in bed, with sore and swollen eyes;
The captain told me, the man who brought them here.
He's next door—the captain—staying as a guest.

Pyrgo. Is *he* well built?

Palae. Go way! I must admit,
You'd be the perfect all-round stallion:
Male or female, all's alike to you.
Back to business!

Pyrgo. That advice you gave me:
I want you to speak to Philocomasium.
You talk the same kind of language, you and she.

Palae. It's better for you to tell her face to face.
Say you simply have to find a wife.
Your family want it; your friends are forcing you.

Pyrgo. You think that's best?

Palae. Of course I think it's best.

Pyrgo. All right, I'll go in. Meanwhile, you wait here;
Keep watch and call to me when *she* comes out.

Palae. Just get on with the job.

Pyrgo. It's as good as done.
If she won't go willingly, I'll kick her out!

Palae. No, no, no! Be careful! She must leave you
With good grace. And give her what I said:
Have her take the gold and trinkets you piled on her.

Pyrgo. I will!

Palae.   I think you'll easily get your way.
            Go in. Don't stand around.

Pyrgo.   Your wish is my command.
                                (exit into house)

Palae.   *(to audience)*
            Well, he doesn't seem to change much, does he?   1130
            Didn't I tell you what a lecherous fellow he was?
            Now I need Acroteleutium
            Or her maid or Pleusicles. Holy Jupiter,
            Opportunity's always on my side!
            The very people I wanted most to see   1135
            Are coming out together from the house next door.

                        Act IV, Scene 4

PLEUSICLES, ACROTELEUTIUM, *and* MILPHIDIPPA *emerge from the old man's*
house.

Acrot.   Follow me, look in every direction:
            We don't want any witnesses.

Milph.   I don't see anyone except him,
            And we want him.

Palae.   And he wants you.

Milph.   How are you doing, master craftsman?

Palae.   Me, master craftsman? Rubbish!

Milph.   Why?

Palae.   Because, compared to you, I'm not
            Fit to hammer a nail in the wall!   1140

Acrot.   Oh, come now! Really!

Palae.   This girl's wicked:

91

She's got wit and a smooth, sharp tongue.
What a sight to see her plane the soldier
Down to size!

Milph.   But he's not finished yet.

Palae. Don't you worry: the whole affair's
Beginning to shape up beautifully.
I hope all of you will just continue
Giving your helpful cooperation.
The soldier himself has gone inside
To ask his little concubine   1145
To leave him and go away with her sister
And mother to Athens.

Pleus.   Oh, great!

Palae. Then, too, there's the gold and the jewelry
That he himself piled on the girl:
He's giving it all as a present, for her
To take away—it was my idea!

Pleus. The whole thing should be very easy
If she's willing and he's eager.

Palae. Don't you know, when you're near the top,
As you're climbing out of a deep well,   1150
That's the time of greatest danger?
From the top you can fall straight down again.
This plan of ours has now arrived
At the top of the well; but if the soldier
Comes to his senses, there's no chance
Of saving it. Now most of all
We must be tricky.

Pleus.   Our side clearly
Has plenty of raw material:
The girls make three . . . you, four . . .
I'm five . . . the old man, six.   1155

Palae. The six of us, I'm quite convinced,
Have such a fund of treachery

That we can tackle any town,
Assault the walls, and lay it low.
Just pay attention.

Acrot.   Well, that's why
We're here, to see if you want anything.

Palae.   Wonderful! You, my dear, I now
Appoint Lieutenant-General.

Acrot.   In general, General, as far as I can,
I'll help you get whatever you want.   1160

Palae.   I want the soldier to be duped
With cleverness, wit, and elegance.

Acrot.   Sweet Castor, General, your commands
Are fun!

Palae.   But do you know how?

Acrot.   Of course! By pretending that
I'm racked with love for him.

Palae.   That's it.

Acrot.   And pretending, because of that love,
To have divorced this husband of mine,
Yearning for marriage with him.

Palae.   O.K.   1165
Just one thing more: say that this house
Belongs to you as part of your dowry,
And that the old man went away
From here after your divorce.
So, when the time comes, *he* won't be afraid
To enter someone else's house.

Acrot.   A good idea.

Palae.   But when he comes out,
I'd like you to stand over there a little;

Pretend to scorn your loveliness,
To feel so ugly compared to him;   1170
Make believe you're overawed
By his magnificence; then go on
To praise his handsome body, his face,
His charming manner, his perfect looks.
Enough instructions?

Acrot.   Yes. Will you
Be satisfied if I hand you back
My piece of work so well worked over
That you can't find any fault?

Palae.   Fair enough. Now, Pleusicles,
Learn the orders I've got for you.   1175
As soon as this job's done and she's
Disappeared inside, that's the time
For you to come along to our house
All dressed up like a sea captain.
Wear a rusty-colored hat,
A woolen patch over one eye,
And also a rusty-colored cloak
(That's a favorite color with sailors)
Hitched up on your left shoulder,
With your other arm waving free.   1180
Be neat and tidy: you must pretend
You're the owner and master of the ship.
This old man will provide the costume;
He's got slaves who are fishermen.

Pleus.   What then? When I'm all dressed up,
Tell me, what do you want me to do?

Palae.   Come here and call for Philocomasium
As if you're acting for her mother.   1185
Tell her, if she's going to Athens,
To go with you quickly to the harbor;
Anything she wants placed aboard
She must have carried to the ship.
Unless she comes, you'll give orders
To sail: the wind is favorable.

Pleus.   This picture pleases me. Go on!

Palae.   At once our friend will encourage her
To go, to hurry up, not keep
Her mother waiting.

Pleus.   You think of everything!   1190

Palae.   I'll tell her to ask for me as a porter
To carry her luggage to the harbor.
He'll order me to go with her
To the harbor. And then (please realize)
I'll leave with you at once for Athens.

Pleus.   And when you've arrived there, before
You've passed three days in slavery,
I'll see that you're a free man.

Palae.   Go quickly and get dressed.

Pleus.   Anything
Else?

Palae.   Remember what I've said.   1195

Pleus.   Goodbye. (*exit stage right*)

Palae.   (*turning to the* WOMEN)
                    You two go inside here
Right now; I'm pretty sure that he
Will soon be coming out this way.

Acrot.   We just *adore* taking orders from you.
(*The* WOMEN *move toward the old man's door.*)

Palae.   Go on, get out of here. Look!
The door's opening right on schedule.
Here he comes, smiling: he's got his way.
He's panting for a fantasy, poor fellow!

Act IV, Scene 5

As the WOMEN *disappear from sight,* PYRGOPOLYNICES *emerges from his own house.*

Pyrgo.   I got my way the way I wanted,
          In a spirit of friendship and goodwill,   1200
          With Philocomasium.

Palae.   Why
          Were you so long inside the house?

Pyrgo.   I've never seen her so in love:
          That girl adores me more than ever!

Palae.   What happened?

Pyrgo.   Oh, how I pleaded with her,
          And oh, what stubborn stuff she was!
          But finally I got my way.
          I gave her all those special presents:
          Some she wanted, some she demanded;
          I made her a present of you as well.   1205

Palae.   Me too? How will I ever
          Live without you?

Pyrgo.   Come, cheer up.
          At the same time I'll give you your freedom.
          I tried hard to see if I could
          Persuade the girl in any way
          To leave me without taking you.
          But she overwhelmed me.

Palae.   I put my trust
          In the gods and you. At any rate,
          Though your news is bitter to me, because
          I must forgo you, the best of masters,   1210
          Still I'm glad that your beauty
          And my help have led to a victory
          Over this woman from next door.
          I'm winning her over for you now.

Pyrgo.   Why waste words? I will make you
          A free man and a wealthy man
          If you can do it.

Palae.   I'll see it's done.

Pyrgo.   I'm burning to get her.

Palae.   Easy does it!
          Control yourself; don't be so passionate!
          Look! Here she is, coming outside.   1215

Act IV, Scene 6

Enter ACROTELEUTIUM *and* MILPHIDIPPA *from the old man's house.*

Milph.   (*sotto voce*) Mistress, look! The soldier's here.

Acrot.   Where?

Milph.   To our left.

Acrot.   I see him.

Milph.   Glance out of the corner of your eye,
          So he won't know we've spotted him.

Acrot.   I see him. Oh, Jupiter! Now's the time
          For us to stoop even lower than usual!

Milph.   You go first.

Acrot.   (*aloud*) I want to know,
          Did you actually meet the man in person?
          (*aside*) Keep your voice up, let him hear.

Milph.   (*aloud*) Yes, by Pollux, I spoke to *him,*   1220
          Calmly, for as long as I wanted,
          Taking my time, pleasing myself.

Pyrgo.   (*sotto voce*) Do you hear what she says?

97

Palae.   Yes, I hear it.
How happy she is to have been with you!

Acrot.   Oh, what a lucky woman you are!

Pyrgo.   They all seem to love me.

Palae.   You deserve it.

Acrot.   Sweet Castor, that's amazing news:
You walked up to him with your request!
They say he's usually approached like a king,
By letter or by courier.   1225

Milph.   Well, I swear I barely had a chance
To approach him with my request.

Palae.   What fame you enjoy among the women!

Pyrgo.   I'll endure it; it's the will of Venus.

Acrot.   To Venus I express my thanks,
To her I speak this heartfelt prayer:
Dear goddess, let me have a chance at him,
The man I love, the man I burn for;
Please make him kind to me, I pray,
Don't let him be cross at what I yearn for.   1230

Milph.   I hope it'll happen, though many girls
Have already set their sights on him.
He spurns them and shuts himself away
From all of them. You're the only exception.

Acrot.   That's why I'm devoured with dread—
Because he's hard to satisfy.
His eyes may cause a change of heart
As soon as he catches sight of me;
Perhaps his savoir-faire will make him
Scorn my appearance on the spot.   1235

Milph.   It won't happen, don't be discouraged!

Pyrgo. See how she belittles herself!

Acrot. I'm worried that your description of me
Made me prettier than I am.

Milph. I was careful to see that you'd
Be lovelier than he thinks you are.

Acrot. Ye gods, if he doesn't want to have me
As his wife, I'll kiss his knees,
Imploring him; otherwise,
If I fail in my request,   1240
I'll kill myself! Life without him?
For me, it's quite impossible.

Pyrgo. I've got to save this girl from death,
I see. Shall I approach?

Palae.   No, no!
Don't you see, you'll cheapen yourself
If you lavish yourself before you're asked.
Let *her* do the asking, let her come
To inquire, to desire, to wait for you.
Let her! Do you want to tarnish
That glory of yours? Please be careful.   1245
This situation's happened only
Twice in human history:
You and Sappho's lover, Phaon—
Both desired to the *n*th degree.[7]

Acrot. Shall I go in, or do you prefer
To call him out, Milphidippa?

Milph. Neither. We should wait here
Till someone comes out.

Acrot.   I can't last
Without going in.

---

[7] There was a legend that the famous poet of Lesbos fell in love with a certain ferryman named Phaon; when he rejected her advances, she hurled herself off a cliff into the sea.

Milph. The door's shut.

Acrot. I'll break it down!

Milph. You're out of your mind! 1250

Acrot. If he has ever been in love,
Or if he's as wise as he is handsome,
Whatever I do in the name of love,
He'll forgive and be merciful.

Palae. Look how this unhappy girl
Is ruined by love!

Pyrgo. The feeling's mutual.

Palae. Quiet, she'll hear you.

Milph. Why have you stopped?
You're looking stunned! Why don't you knock?

Acrot. (*slowly, in a trance*) Not within is the one I want.

Milph. How do you know?

Acrot. My nose . . . knows. 1255
It would sniff . . . a whiff . . . if
He were there.

Pyrgo. Now she's psychic!
Because she loves me, therefore Venus
Has made her the gift of prophecy!

Acrot. Somewhere here, not far away,
Is the man I long to see: he smells!

Pyrgo. Holy Pollux, her nose has better
Vision than her eyes!

Palae. She's blind with love.

Acrot. (*in distress*) Hold me up, please!

Milph.   Why?

Acrot.   So I
Won't fall.

Milph.   What is it?

Acrot.   I can't stand up;   1260
My eyes have caused my mind to fail.

Milph.   Holy Pol, you must have seen . . .
The soldier!

Acrot.   Yes.

Milph.   I don't see him. Where is he?

Acrot.   Oh, you'd see him if you loved him.

Milph.   I swear you don't love him any more
Than I would, dear lady, if you'd let me.

Palae.   All the girls certainly love you,
The moment they get a glimpse of you.

Pyrgo.   I may have told you some time or other:
Venus is my father's mother.   1265

Acrot.   Dear Milphidippa, please go up
To him and meet him.

Pyrgo.   She's afraid of me!

Palae.   (*aloud*) She's coming to *us*.

Milph.   It's *you* I want.

Pyrgo.   And *we* want *you*!

Milph.   Just as you ordered,
I've brought my mistress out of doors.

Pyrgo.   So I see.

Milph.   Well, tell her to approach.

Pyrgo.   I've taught my heart not to despise her
Like other women; you asked so nicely.

Milph.   Mercy, she won't be able to speak
A word, if she comes near you.   1270
While she merely gazed from afar,
Her eyes cut off the tip of her tongue.

Pyrgo.   This woman's illness must be cured,
I see.

Milph.   Look! She's trembling: terror struck her
When she caught a glimpse of you.

Pyrgo.   Even brave warriors act that way;
Don't be surprised that a woman should.
But what does she want me to do?

Milph.   To come to her house: with you
She wants to live and spend a lifetime.   1275

Pyrgo.   I, come to her house? Well, she's married!
Her husband would catch me in the act.

Milph.   No! For your sake she drove out her husband.

Pyrgo.   How in the world could she do that?

Milph.   This house is part of her dowry.

Pyrgo.   Is it?

Milph.   Yes.

Pyrgo.   Tell her to go inside.
I'll be there presently.

Milph.   Just see

That you don't keep her waiting long:
It would be mental cruelty.

Pyrgo. I won't,
Believe me. Get going.

Milph. We're going. 1280
(*They hurry into the old man's house.*)

Pyrgo. What's this I see?

Palae. What do you see?

Pyrgo. Somebody's coming along here
(Look!) in the uniform of a sailor.

Palae. He's coming to us; he must want you.
This is the ship's captain.

Pyrgo. I suppose
He's coming to fetch *her* now.

Palae. I guess so.

Act IV, Scene 7

Enter PLEUSICLES, *stage right, supposedly from the harbor. He speaks first to the audience.*

Pleus. If I didn't know that love had caused other men
To act disgracefully, I'd be more ashamed 1285
To be parading here, for love, in this get-up.
But I've been told that many men, for love,
Have done many things dishonorable and unworthy.
Take Achilles: the way he let his friends get killed—
But there's Palaestrio, standing with the soldier; 1290
Now I must declaim a different speech.

(*in a loud "soliloquy"*)
Women are born daughters of Delay,
When you're waiting for a woman, any other

            Kind of delay, however long, seems trivial.
            I think they practice being slow!   1295

            I'll call for this Philocomasium. I'll knock
            On the door. Hey! Anyone here?

Palae.   Young man, what is it?
            Why are you knocking?

Pleus.   I'm looking for Philocomasium.
            I'm from her mother. She'd better come, if she's coming.
            She's holding everyone up: we want to sail.   1300

Pyrgo.   Things have been ready for ages. Palaestrio,
            Take the gold, jewelry, clothing, all her treasures,
            And get slaves to help you carry them to the ship.
            All the presents I gave are packed: let her take them!

Palae.   Yes sir. (*exit into the soldier's house*)

Pleus.   Oh Herc, please hurry.

Pyrgo.   He won't delay.   1305
            What's that thing there? What happened to your eye?

Pleus.   My eye's all *right*.

Pyrgo.   I mean your *left*.

Pleus.   I'll tell you.
            Because of my love, I can't see out of this eye;
            If I'd steered away from my love, it would see quite well.

            They're holding me up too long.

Pyrgo.   Look, here they are.   1310

Act IV, Scene 8

Enter PALAESTRIO *and* PHILOCOMASIUM *from the soldier's house.* PHILO-
COMASIUM *is in tears, and continues to sob as the scene develops.*

Palae. Oh please, won't you ever stop your crying
Today?

Philo.   How can I help crying?
I'm leaving the place where my life was most
Beautiful.

Palae.   See! Here's the man
Who's come from your mother and your sister.

Philo. I see him.

Pyrgo.   Palaestrio, do you hear?

Palae. What do you want?

Pyrgo.   Get those things
Brought out: all the presents I gave her.

Pleus. How do you do, Philocomasium.

Philo. How do you do.

Pleus.   Your mother and sister   1315
Asked me to give their love to you.

Philo. Then give them my love, too.

Pleus. They ask you to come, while the wind
Is right, so they can get under way;
If your mother hadn't been sick,
They would have come along with me.

Philo. I'll go, though it's not what I want to do:
My sense of duty—

Pleus.   Wise girl!

Pyrgo. If she hadn't lived with me,
She'd still be a stupid girl today.   1320

Philo. I'm simply tortured by the fact

That I'll be removed from the sort of man
Who can make any girl in the world
Overflow with cleverness.
Also, because I was close to you,
My heart grew wilder all the time.
And now, it seems, I must give up
That glory.

Pyrgo.   Don't cry.

Philo.   I can't help it
When I look at you.

Pyrgo.   Come on, cheer up!

Philo.   I'm the only one who knows how it hurts!   1325

Palae.   I don't wonder, Philocomasium,
That you were glad to be in this house,
Or that *his* beauty, character, courage
Won your heart and held you here.
I'm just a slave; but I weep too
At the sight of him, because we're parting.

Philo.   Please, may I have a last embrace
Before I leave you?

Pyrgo.   Yes, you may.

Philo.   Oh, my dearest! Oh, my darling!

(*Hurling herself at* PYRGOPOLYNICES, *she slips past him and faints into* PLEUSICLES' *arms.*)

Palae.   Watch out there! Catch the woman,   1330
Don't let her hurt herself.

Pyrgo.   What's going on?

Palae.   Because she's leaving you, she's fainted
Suddenly, unhappy girl.

Pyrgo.   Run inside and bring some water!

Palae.   Water's no good; rest is what
She needs. Don't interfere, please,
Until she comes around again.

Pyrgo.   They've got their heads too close together.
I don't like it! Take your lips away
From hers, sailor; you're looking for trouble!   1335

Pleus.   I was checking to see if she was breathing.

Pyrgo.   Well, you should have used your ear!

Pleus.   If you prefer, I'll drop her.

Pyrgo.   Oh, no!
Hang on!

Palae.   (*aside*) I'm getting uncomfortable.

Pyrgo.   Slaves! Go and fetch from the house
All the presents I gave this girl.

Palae.   (*to the statue of Pyrgopolynices' Lar*)
Hail to thee, dear household god!
Take my last greeting before I go.
Dear fellow slaves, both men and women,
Goodbye, good luck to all of you!   1340
I pray you'll all speak well of me,
Even when I'm far away.

Pyrgo.   Come, Palaestrio, cheer up!

Palae.   Oh dear, I can't help crying
Now that I'm leaving!

Pyrgo.   Take it easy!

Palae.   I'm the only one who knows how it hurts!

Philo. *Oh!* What happened? What's going on?
What do I see? Hail, light of day!

Pleus. Hail, yourself! Are you better now?

Philo. Oh, tell me, whom have I embraced?   1345
What man? I'm ruined! Am I myself?

Pleus. Don't be frightened . . . my lovely one!
(*They embrace again.*)

Pyrgo. What does that business mean?

Palae.   Remember,
The woman has recently been unconscious.
(*aside to* PLEUSICLES) I'm very much afraid that this
Will finally get too obvious.

Pyrgo.   (*overhearing*) What will?

Palae. (*improvising*) Having all these presents
Carried behind us through the city;
I'm afraid you'll be criticized for this.

Pyrgo. It's my stuff, not theirs, I'm giving away.   1350
I couldn't care less for them! All right,
Go, and may all the gods attend you!

Palae. I mention it only for your sake.

Pyrgo.   Of course.

Palae. And now, goodbye.

Pyrgo.   Goodbye to you.

Palae. Go ahead, I'll follow you soon;
I want a few words with master.

(PLEUSICLES, PHILOCOMASIUM, *and the* SLAVES *leave for the harbor,
stage right.* PALAESTRIO *is alone with* PYRGOPOLYNICES.)

Palae.   Though you've always held other
Slaves more faithful to you than me,
All the same, for you I feel
Nothing but thanks for everything.   1355
If you had willed it so, I'd much
Prefer to be a slave for you
Than to live free with someone else.

Pyrgo.   Please keep your courage up.

Palae.   Ohhh, when the thought occurs to me
How I'll have to change my habits:
Learning a woman's way of life,
Forgetting military routine!

Pyrgo.   There, there, be a good fellow!

Palae.   I can't
Do it; I've lost all desire.   1360

Pyrgo.   Go on, follow them, don't delay.

Palae.   Goodbye.

Pyrgo.   Goodbye to you.

Palae.   And please (you will remember, won't you?),
If I do obtain my freedom
I'll send word to you—don't
Let me down.[8]

Pyrgo.   That's not in my nature.

Palae.   Keep reflecting, whatever you do,
How faithful I've always been to you.
In this way you'll come to know
Who's your friend and who's your foe.   1365

---

[8]Palaestrio has been promised his freedom in lines 1207 and 1213. Here he is reminding Pyrgopolynices that a former master has a continuing obligation to assist his freedman, by establishing a patron-client relationship.

Pyrgo.	Yes, in the past I've often seen it;
	Now I know you really mean it.

Palae.	You know? Well, sir, after today
	You'll swear to the truth of what I say.

Pyrgo.	I can scarcely refrain from ordering you
	To stay here.

Palae.   Oh, you mustn't do that!
People would say that you're a liar,
That you have no sense of honor,
That I'm the only one of your slaves
With any real loyalty.   1370
If I thought that there was a way
Of doing it honorably, I'd urge you;
But it's quite impossible. Please don't do it.

Pyrgo. Well, go.

Palae.   I'll endure whatever comes.

Pyrgo. Goodbye, then.

Palae.   I really must
Go . . . quickly. (*exit stage right*)

Pyrgo.   Goodbye, goodbye.
Before he did this, I always thought
This fellow was my very worst slave;
Now I discover he's faithful to me.
When I think a bit about it,   1375
I was a fool to send him off!
But now I'll go inside the house
To my lovely lady. Just a moment:
I think I heard a noise at the door.

Act IV, Scene 9

A youthful SLAVE *comes out of the old man's house.*

Slave (*over his shoulder*)
Don't keep prompting me, I remember my job.
I'll go and find him now, wherever he is;
I'll track him down, I won't spare any pains.   1380

Pyrgo. He's looking for me. I'll go and meet the lad.

Slave Ah, there you are. Hail, loveliest of men,
Abounding in astounding charm, uniquely
Loved by two gods.

Pyrgo.   Which two?

Slave   Mars and Venus.

Pyrgo. A clever lad!

Slave   She begs you to go inside.   1385
She wants you, needs you, waits with bated breath.
Help one who loves you. Don't stand there, go in!

Pyrgo.   I will!
                    (*exit into the old man's house*)

Slave All by himself he's snared himself in the net.
The trap is ready: the old man's manning his post,
To attack our battle-shy adulterer,   1390
Who thinks all women adore him at first sight,
Though in fact he's loathed by men and women alike.
Now I'll enter the turmoil; I hear shouting.
                    (*exit into the old man's house*)

ACT V

Amid great commotion, enter PERIPLECTOMENUS, *followed from his house by* PYRGOPOLYNICES, *who is threatened by burly* SLAVES *and by a menacing cook named* CARIO.

Act V, Scene 1

Perip.	Bring him here! If he won't come Pick him up and throw him out! Hang him up halfway between Heaven and earth! Tear him apart!	1395

Pyrgo. I beg you, Periplectomenus, by Hercules!

Perip. By Hercules, you're wasting breath.
Cario, how's your carving knife?
You must be sure it's really sharp.

Cario Oh, it's been itching to get this lecher!
Lippety-lop: loin chop!
I'll slice away and hang the bits
Like babies' beads around his neck.

Pyrgo. I'm finished!

Perip.   Not yet! There's more to come.

Cario	Now do you want me to fly at the fellow?	1400

Perip. No. First he should be pounded
With clubs.

Cario   Yes. Repeatedly!

Perip. How dare you! Why did you try to seduce
   Another man's wife? Shame on you!

Pyrgo. So help me gods, I didn't invite her;
   She just came.

Perip.   He's lying; hit him.

Pyrgo. Wait! Let me speak!

Perip. (*to his* SLAVES) What are you waiting for?

Pyrgo. Please may I say something?

Perip. Say it.

Pyrgo.   I was asked to go to her.

Perip. And you dared to go? This will teach you!   1405

Pyrgo. *Oh! ow!* Now I'm pounded
   Enough! Oh, please!

Cario   How soon do I slice?

Perip. Whenever you like. With all your strength,
   Strain him and stretch him out full length.

Pyrgo. Holy Hercules! Listen to me
   Before you let him cut me up.

Perip. Speak.

Pyrgo.   I had some justification.
   I thought that she was unattached.
   This is what the woman told me,
   Her maid, who was our go-between.   1410

Perip. Say you won't take vengeance (swear!)
   On any man in this affair,
   For beatings you've received today,

> Or future beatings, come what may,
> If we don't perform this operation,
> Venus' darling little relation.

Pyrgo.   By Jupiter and Mars I swear
    I'll hurt no man in this affair
    Merely because I'm black and blue:
    Justice demanded it of you.   1415
    If my testimonials aren't attacked,
    I'll be getting off easily, in fact.

Perip.   And if you break your oath, what then?

Pyrgo.   May they never testify again!

Cario   I think he should be beaten up
    And then we ought to let him go.

Pyrgo.   May all the gods in heaven bless you!
    My dearest friend! My advocate!

Cario   O.K., my fee: a hundred drachmas.

Pyrgo.   What for?

Cario   To let you leave today   1420
    With good testimonials,
    Darling little grandson of Venus.
    You won't get away otherwise,
    Make no mistake.

Pyrgo.   All right.

Cario   You're learning.
    In case you're worried about your tunic,
    Cloak, and sword, they'll be safe with us.

Slave   Do I keep on pounding, or have I hit him
    Often enough?

Pyrgo.   I've been softened enough
    With those clubs of yours. Please!

Perip.	Release	
	This man.	

Pyrgo.	Oh, thank you, sir.	1425

Perip. If, at any time in the future,
I catch you here: no testimonials!

Pyrgo. I'm not arguing with that!

Perip. Let's go inside, Cario.

(*Exit* PERIPLECTOMENUS, *with* CARIO *and the* SLAVES. PYRGO-
POLYNICES *is left alone momentarily, until his* SLAVES *enter from the
harbor.*)

Pyrgo. Look! Here are my slaves. Tell me,
Has Philocomasium left already?

Slave Long ago.

Pyrgo.   *Ah! oh!!*

Slave   You'd say much more
Than that, if you knew what I know.
You see, the man who had the patch
Over his eye wasn't really a sailor.   1430

Pyrgo. Then who was he?

Slave   Philocomasium's
Lover.

Pyrgo. How do you know?

Slave   I know.
As soon as they passed the city gate,
Right there, without a moment's pause,
They were kissing in each other's arms.

Pyrgo. *Alas!* Unhappy me!
I can see that I've been tricked.

That crook of a man, Palaestrio—
He swindled me and sucked me in.

(*directly to the audience*)
I find that justice has been done: 1435
If more adulterers met my fate,
There'd be less adultery in the state;
Illicit affairs wouldn't even be planned!

Let's all go home now. Give us a hand.

(*exeunt omnes*)

PSEUDOLUS

Introduction to *Pseudolus*

Pseudolus was first performed in 191 B.C., at the festival held in honor of the Great Mother; it is one of only two Plautine comedies for which we have an ancient production notice or *didascalia* (the other is *Stichus*). Nothing is known about the Greek model on which it was based. Composed late in Plautus' career, *Pseudolus* shows the comic playwright in top form. Although this work is not as carefully constructed as, say, *Rudens,* it is unsurpassed for comic invention of the peculiarly Plautine kind. A hit from the time of its first performance, it was still popular in Cicero's day, well over a century later, when the role of Ballio was being played by the celebrated actor Quintus Roscius.

The play's greatest strength, perhaps, is its magnificent gallery of characters, all stock types from the tradition of New Comedy, but each a graphic individual. The Roman stage has no more memorable a lovesick adolescent than Calidorus, whose desperate passion for a high-priced young slave-girl establishes the comic situation. Calidorus is a delightfully appealing young man, hopelessly inept and dependent on the family slave, Pseudolus ("Trickster"). His father Simo is the gruff and severe type of old man, the ideal target for a scheme of deception; yet in the final analysis Simo proves to be fair-minded and capable even of laughing at himself.

The more tolerant and amiable type of *senex* can be seen in the person of Callipho, the next-door neighbor. For some mysterious reason, either Plautus or his Greek predecessor chose to have this character disappear abruptly at the end of Act I, to be replaced by a much younger counterpart named Charinus. Elsewhere in the play, we meet a rather dull-witted messenger slave named Harpax ("Snatch"), agent of the braggart warrior who is Calidorus' rival for the girl. As well, we meet a devious slave named Simia ("Monkey"), whose ready wit and cunning are crucial to the main deception. We also encounter an unusually garrulous and inventive cook, a type well established on the Greek stage, but often given greater prominence in Plautus by means of comic embellishments.[1]

Vivid and colorful though they may be, all these characters are dwarfed by the two figures who dominate the action of the play—the pimp Ballio and the crafty slave Pseudolus.

Strictly speaking, we should not use the word "pimp" to translate the Latin term *leno,* which denoted a slave merchant who specialized in selling beautiful young women. However unacceptable we may find his profession today, he was a legitimate businessman in ancient Rome. Still, he did play the role of procurer, renting call girls to clients at large (see Ballio's outrageous roll call, lines 173–229). Moreover, he was regarded, on the Roman stage at least, as such a shady and disreputable character that the modern label of pimp may appropriately reflect his public esteem. Ballio is the most villainous and unprincipled representative of his profession in all of ancient comedy. Plautus depicts him with such hyperbolic glee that we may be willing to overlook the offensive nature of a comic situation where women appear only as mute sexual merchandise. (Calidorus' beloved Phoenicium does have a voice of sorts, even if it is only in a letter, read aloud by Pseudolus.) Ballio's extended polymetric song in Act I is a brilliant poetic composition, far longer (we can be certain) than anything Plautus would have found in his Greek original. The entire characterization (Roscius' choice of part, we should recall) is a comic *tour de force.*

Nonetheless it is Pseudolus to whom the play belongs, in more ways than one. In size and importance, his is the most taxing and dominant of any Plautine principal role. Almost continuously on stage, Pseudolus assumes control over all the other characters, steering and coaxing the plot through each tortuous turn. Like the wily slave Palaestrio, his forerunner in *Miles Gloriosus,* he will often resort to military imagery in order to extol his prowess. His most apposite metaphors, however, are drawn from the world of the stage. Plautus virtually convinces us that Pseudolus, the grand master of improvisation, is making up the plot as he goes along: this slave-hero, so we believe, is starring in a comedy of his own creation.[2] Confirming this impression, Pseudolus serves his audience a continual diet of theatrical criticism, offering a running commentary on the action that he has invented. He has no fewer than seven formal soliloquies, and countless other pointed asides.

As one might expect of a fast-paced, "improvised" story line, there are

---

[1] See J. C. B. Lowe, "Cooks in Plautus," *Classical Antiquity* 4 (1985): 72–102; and "The Cook Scene of Plautus' *Pseudolus,*" *Classical Quarterly* 35 (1985): 411–416.

[2] For a stimulating essay on this theme, see the chapter "Words, Words, Words" in Niall W. Slater's *Plautus in Performance* (Princeton, 1985).

several flaws and inconsistencies of plot. Why, for example, is Calidorus surprised in Act I, Scene 3 to hear about Phoenicium's sale to the Macedonian soldier, when he has bewailed that circumstance in Act I, Scene 1? What happens to Callipho, for whom Pseudolus (lines 547–560) has planned a key role? Again, what happens to the dinner that is being so elaborately prepared by the zany cook? And how exactly are we to explain the play's curious financial transactions, whereby a sum of twenty minas is passed in circular fashion from hand to hand? These problems can be addressed and resolved, if one wishes to take them seriously;[3] but it is unlikely that any of them will even be noticed in the frenetic pace of performance.

For two generations, the standard English-language edition of this comedy has been Edgar H. Sturtevant's *T. Macci Plauti Pseudolus* (New Haven: Yale University Press, 1932). Though still useful, it has now been superseded by the excellent edition and commentary of M. M. Willcock, *Plautus: Pseudolus* (Bristol: Bristol Classical Press, and Oak Park, Ill.: Bolchazy-Carducci, 1987). Willcock provides a very convenient bibliography.

[3] See Willcock (cited in the final paragraph), pp. 15–17.

CHARACTERS

PSEUDOLUS	a cunning slave
CALIDORUS	his master's teenaged son
BALLIO	a slave dealer and pimp
SIMO	Calidorus' father, a stern old man
CALLIPHO	Simo's friend, a tolerant old man
HARPAX	an officer's slave
CHARINUS	a young man, Calidorus' friend
SIMIA	a cunning slave
YOUNG SLAVE	an unnamed slave of Ballio's
COOK	anonymous, but not reticent
COURTESANS	Ballio's female slaves; silent roles
ATTENDANT SLAVES	minor or silent roles

PROLOGUE

You'd better rise and stretch your legs,
Walk up and down the aisle;
Here comes a Plautine comedy,
It's bound to last a while.[4]

---

[4]Our manuscripts of Plautus contain this snippet of verse—two lines of Latin. It appears to be a fragment of a prologue composed for a revival of *Pseudolus,* sometime after Plautus' death. If Plautus' original play contained a prologue, it has been lost without a trace.

ACT I

The stage depicts three adjacent houses on a street in Athens. In the center is Simo's residence, flanked by the houses of his wealthy neighbor Callipho (stage right) and the disreputable pimp Ballio (stage left). As the play opens, the slave PSEUDOLUS *and his young master,* CALIDORUS, *emerge from Simo's front door.*

PSEUDOLUS *wears the bizarre stock costume of the cunning slave—his physical appearance will be graphically described later in the play.* CALIDORUS *is a typical lovesick adolescent—a handsome, well-dressed, well-mannered, and appealing youth. Though he is not unintelligent, he is predictably unresourceful and naive. He is now preoccupied with the scrutiny of folding wooden letter-tablets, a standard form of ancient correspondence.*

Act I, Scene 1

Pseud.   Master, if only I could read your mind
And learn the torture that's tormenting you,
I'd gladly spare two men a lot of bother: 5
I wouldn't need to ask, or you to answer.
Now, since that's impossible, necessity
Compels me to question you. Answer me this:
Why have you been acting half-alive
These last few days, toting letter-tablets
Everywhere and drenching them with tears,   10
Taking no one into your confidence?
(*heroically*) Give voice, that I may know what I know not.

Calid.   Oh, Pseudolus, I'm suffering!

Pseud.   Jupiter forbid!

Calid.   It's out of Jupiter's control;
Venus rules the region of my pain.   15

Pseud.   Am I allowed some knowledge? In the past,
         You've made me privy-partner of your plans.

Calid.   My attitude's unchanged.

Pseud.   Then state your problem.
         I can offer cash, concern, or kind advice.

Calid.   (*handing him the tablets*)
         Take this message; learn for yourself   20
         Why I am quite consumptified with gloom and worry.

Pseud.   As you wish. (*examining tablets*) But oh! what's this?

Calid.   What is it?

Pseud.   I think these letters must be sexy characters:
         They're climbing all over each other.

Calid.   Very funny.

Pseud.   Holy Pol, unless the Sibyl reads this first,   25
         No one else could ever decipher it.

Calid.   Why are you so rude to charming letters,
         Charming tablets, traced with a charming hand?

Pseud.   Excuse me, sir; do chickens now have hands?
         These are hen-tracts.

Calid.   Oh, you make me sick.   30
         Read it or hand it back.

Pseud.   All right, I'll read.
         Take heart.

Calid.   My heart is lost.

Pseud.   Well, find it again!

Calid.	No, I'll keep quiet; find it yourself in the wax.
	That's where my heart resides—my breast is vacant now.
Pseud.	(*suddenly*) I see your girl friend, Calidorus.
Calid.	(*startled*) Where is she? Where? 35
Pseud.	(*pointing to her name*)
	Here, stretched out upon the boards, relaxed in wax.
Calid.	(*furious*) May the gods all smother you—
Pseud.	—with happiness.
Calid.	(*tragically*)
	My life's been brief, like a blade of summer grass:
	Sudden was my birth, and suddenly I'm gone.
Pseud.	Shut up, I'm trying to read.
Calid.	Why not begin? 40
Pseud.	(*reading*)
	"Phoenicium to her darling Calidorus:
	With wax and string and these appealing characters
	I wish you love and health; your healing love I beg.
	My eyes are moist, my heart and soul are faltering."
Calid.	I'm sunk, Pseudolus! I can't find the healing love 45
	To send her back.
Pseud.	What healing love?
Calid.	The silver kind.
Pseud.	(*waving the tablets*)
	You're willing to repay her wooden love
	With silver? Keep your wits about you, please!
Calid.	Read on, and soon the letter will explain
	How urgently that silver must be found. 50

Pseud.   "My pimp has sold me to a foreigner
(A Macedonian military man)
For twenty silver minas, dearest love.
Before that soldier left, he paid out fifteen
In advance. Now there's a balance of only five.
Therefore the soldier left a token here,   55
A portrait wax impression from his ring,
And so, when someone brings a token like it,
I'm to be sent with him at once. A day is set
For the transaction: next Dionysia."

Calid.   And that's tomorrow! I'm on the brink of doom,   60
Unless you've help to offer.

Pseud.   Let me finish.

Calid.   Yes! I feel as though I'm talking with her.
Read—you give me bittersweet delight.

Pseud.   (*reading again, with increasing fervor*)
"Now our loves, our lives, our passionate embraces,
Laughter, fun, sweet talk, and sexy face-to-faces,   65
Slender little hips and thighs a-jiggle,
Tender little lips and tongues a-wiggle,
Juicy jousts of bouncy-boob and titty-tickle—
All our hopes of orgiastic consummation
Face dismemberment, disaster, desolation,   70
If we fail to find some mutual salvation.
Everything I know I've tried to tell you clearly:
Now I'll put you to the test. One question, merely:
Are you in love or just pretending?
                      Yours sincerely."

Calid.   An awful letter, Pseudolus.

Pseud.   Absolutely awful!

Calid.   Why aren't you crying?

Pseud.   I've got stony eyes; I can't   75
Implore them to spit out a single tear.

Calid. How's that?

Pseud.   Hereditary dry-eye-itis.

Calid. Won't you help me just a little?

Pseud.   What should I do?

Calid. *Oh, dear!*

Pseud.   "Oh, dear"? Great Herc, no need to scrimp
In that department; go ahead.

Calid. I'm so depressed, I can't find any cash to borrow—   80

Pseud. *Oh, dear!*

Calid.   There's not a penny in the house—

Pseud.   *Oh, dear!*

Calid. He's going to carry off my girl tomorrow—

Pseud.   *Oh, dear!*

Calid. Do you really think that helps?

Pseud.   I give what I've got:
I have an inexhaustible supply of groans.

Calid. It's all over for me today. But can you lend me   85
A single drachma I'd pay back tomorrow?

Pseud. Hardly—not if my life were on the line.
What will you do with a drachma?

Calid.   Buy a rope.

Pseud. What for?

Calid.   To help me learn to swing. (*tragically*) I plan,
Ere shadows fall, to fall among the shades.   90

| Pseud. | Then who'll pay back the drachma that I gave you?
| | Is that why you want to hang yourself, you sneak,
| | To dun me out of the drachma I've donated?

Calid.   There's just no way that I can go on living
         If she is grabbed from me and granted to another.   95
         (*bursts into tears*)

Pseud.   Why cry, you cuckoo? You'll survive.

Calid.   I've got to cry:
         I haven't any money of my own,
         No hope on earth of scraping up a scrap.

Pseud.   If I caught the drift of the lady's billet-doux,
         Your eyes have got to shower silver tears,   100
         Or this pretentious crying act will help
         As much as catching raindrops in a sieve.
         Don't fear, my lovesick dear, I won't desert you.
         Somewhere, somehow, some way (maybe) today
         I'll find you silvery succor and salvation.   105
         Where, oh where will it come from? I don't know,
         But I know it will: I've got a twitching brow.

Calid.   I only hope your deeds can match your words!

Pseud.   Holy Herc! If once I bang my holy gong,
         You know the holy rumpus I can raise!   110

Calid.   You're now the repository of all my hopes.

Pseud.   Is it enough if I get this girl for you today
         As your very own, or if I give you twenty minas?

Calid.   It's enough—if it happens.

Pseud.   Demand your twenty minas,
         So you'll know I'll carry out my promise to you.   115
         Make it all quite legal: I'm itching to take the oath.

Calid.   (*formally*)
         Sir, this day will you give me twenty minas?

130

Pseud.	Sir, I will. And now don't be a nuisance.
	Listen to this, if you still have any doubts:
	If all else fails, I'll pinch it from your papa.

120

Calid.	God save you, I love you! But look: if possible,
	For goodness' sake, put the pinch on Mother, too.

Pseud.	Dispel these worries from your fevered nose.

Calid.	My fevered brain, do you mean?

Pseud.	I hate clichés.
	(*hailing the audience*)
	Now hear ye, hear ye! Lend an ear, ye!

125

These are my solemn words of public warning
For the throng assembled here this morning,
All the citizens by tribe enrolled,
All my acquaintances and friends of old:
If you should meet me, be on guard today,
And don't believe a single word I say.

Calid.	(*startled by a noise from Ballio's house*)
	Shh!
	Sweet Hercules, keep quiet!

Pseud.	Why, what's up?

130

Calid.	The pimp's front door just gave a squeaking noise.

Pseud.	I'd rather twist his legs to make *him* squeak.

Calid.	He's coming out in person: Lord of Lies!

Act I, Scene 2

As PSEUDOLUS *and* CALIDORUS *make themselves inconspicuous,* BALLIO *emerges from his house, wielding a whip; the villainous slave dealer is berating a number of cowering male* SLAVES, *who are his household servants and personal attendants.*

Ballio	Get out! Come on, get out, you slugs!

131

As merchandise you're rotten;
You never do no good nohow:
    There's naught you've not forgotten!
Unless I whip you up this way,
    You aren't the least bit useful;   135
You're more like donkeys than like men,
    With ribs all striped and bruiseful.

(*to audience*) Flog 'em, you'll be the one to cry;
These whipper-slappers always try,
If given the chance, to have their fun:
Grab, swipe, snitch, snatch, eat, drink, and run!
That's just their nature; that's their way.
And so, believe me when I say
You'd rather wolves control your flock
Than have these thugs patrol your block.   140

It isn't always true, you know,
    That seeing is believing;
Though their appearances aren't bad,
    Their actions are deceiving.

(*turning back to the* SLAVES)
Now unless you obey my command, all you guys,
If you don't wipe the sleepiness out of your eyes,
    I'll embroider your hips
    With such colorful strips   145
You'll resemble bright linen embroidered for feasts,
Alexandrian coverlets covered with beasts.

I issued orders yesterday,
Your provinces were all assigned;
But you're such crooked characters,
So careless, so devoid of mind,
You can't remember any job
Without a swift kick from behind.   150
    Perhaps you hope to get so tough
    That my whip won't be hard enough.

(*to audience*) Just look at that! No concentration.
(*cracking his whip at the* SLAVES)

Pay attention, look this way!
Make sure you point your ears at me,
You whip-lashed human specimens!
Your backsides can't get any harder
Than this rawhide whip of mine.
(*flicking his whip at various victims*)
How now? That hurt? There! That's what's done
If any slave shows disrespect.   155

Now form a line in front of me
And pay attention to my words.
(*pointing to a* SLAVE)
You with the jug: go fetch some water;
Fill the kettle for the cook.
(*to another*) You with the axe: you'll oversee
The Province of Woodsplittia.

Slave   This axe is dull.

Ballio   What if it is?
You're not so very sharp yourself.
Do I enjoy your service less
Because you're blunted with my blows?   160
(*to another*) Your task is cleaning up the house.
You know the job. Hurry up! Go in!
(*to another*) Be thou the Keeper of the Couch.
(*to another*) You get to wash the silver plate.

Make sure these jobs are done when I
Return from town; I want to find
That everything's been swept and sprinkled,
Cleaned and leveled, washed and shined.
Today's my birthday, don't you see?
You all must celebrate with me.   165

Throw ham and pork-rind in the pot,
Get sweetbreads, sow-tits boiling hot!
I want to throw a banquet which
Will make the powerful think I'm rich.
Go in and quickly work away;
When cook comes, we want no delay.

(*Except for one personal* ATTENDANT, *Ballio's male* SLAVES *now enter the house.*)

I'm off to market, where I wish
To buy the market out of fish.
Lead on, my boy, and guard your back:
Let no one grab my money sack.   170

Just wait! It nearly slipped my mind
There's something else I've got to do.
You women! Listen to me please:
My next announcement is for you.

(*Ballio's contingent of lovely* LADIES *files out of his house in response to his call.*)[5]

All you who live the languid life
Of dissipation and decay,
Famed mistresses of mighty men,
I'll learn your preference today:
Choose gluttony or liberty;
Siestas or self-interest.   175
Which girls I free and which I sell
I'll find out by a simple test.
Make sure I'm loaded down with loot
From lover-boys that you delight.
Bring in a full year's keep today
Or work the street tomorrow night.

Today's my birthday, as you know.
Bring on the lads who find you fun,
Who call you "sweetheart," "dearest darling,"
"Smoochie-pooch" or "honey-bun."   180
    Make sure they march up by platoon,
    Each bearing a beautiful birthday boon.

Why do I give you clothing, jewelry,
    Everything you need,
When you repay me with obnoxious

---

[5] The roll call of the call girls is perhaps a Plautine expansion on the Greek original. The scene could be staged with the women present from the start.

Drunkenness and greed?
You soak and guzzle, getting high,
While I sit soberly and cry.

So now I'm going to call your names,
Proceeding one by one;   185
Don't try to tell me, by and by,
If any job's undone,
That tasks have not been all assigned.
Attention, everyone!

I'll start with you, Delectium,[6]
The darling of the grain suppliers.
All your lovers own vast stores
Of golden wheat piled mountain high.
Get grain delivered to us, please,
For me and all my household staff—   190
Enough to see us through the year.
Bring me such wheaty affluence
The citizens will change my name
From Ballio, the pauper pimp,
To Jason, prince of opulence.
                              (*exit* DELECTIUM)

Calid.   (*to* PSEUDOLUS) You hear this jailbird chattering?
         He's quite a loudmouth, don't you think?

Pseud.   Dear Pollux, yes! A foulmouth, too.
         Be quiet, though, and listen on!   195

Ballio   Obscenium, your patrons are
         The butchers, rivals of the pimps:
         They make their living, just like us,
         By selling poor and tainted meat.[7]

---

[6]Plautus gives Ballio's courtesans the Greek names of Hedylium ("Sweetie"), Aeschrodora ("Dirty Present"), Xystilis ("Workout"), and Phoenicium ("Rosie"). Though I prefer not to anglicize Plautine proper names, I have turned the first three into Delectium, Obscenium, and Gymnasium (the name of a Plautine call girl in *Cistellaria*.) I have not tampered with Phoenicium, because she is a central (if silent) character.

[7]This joke substitutes for an untranslatable Latin pun. In the next sentence, there is a mythical reference to the wicked Dirce, who was tied to the horns of a bull by Amphion and Zethus, twin sons of Zeus and Antiope.

Unless I get three meat-racks jammed
With juicy carcasses today,
Tomorrow I'll copy what was done
To Dirce by the sons of Jove:
They bound her to a raging bull;
I'll stretch you on an empty meat-rack.   200
                    (*exit* OBSCENIUM)

Pseud. (*to* CALIDORUS) This person makes me blazing mad!
To think the manly youth of Athens
Let him go on living here!
Where do they hide, those lusty lads
Who get their loving from a pimp?
Why don't they meet and all combine
To rid our public of these pests?
But hey, no way!
I've been too simple, too naive.
Where would they get the nerve to hurt
The men their love enslaves them to?   205
Their passion keeps them all from doing
Things their pimps would not approve.

Calid. Be quiet!

Pseud.   Why?

Calid.   You bother me
When you drown out this fellow's words.

Pseud. Then I'll shut up.

Calid.   I wish you would,
Instead of saying that you will.

Ballio It's your turn now, Gymnasium,
All of whose lover-boys possess   210
Untold reserves of olive oil.
If oil's not dumped in leather sacks
And carried here to me forthwith,
I'll have *you* dumped in a leather sack
And carried to the whorehouse shed.

There you'll be issued with a couch
Where you will get no sleep, but where,   215
To the point of sheer exhaustion. . . . Do you
Get the drift of my remarks?

[See here, you snake! When you've so many
Boyfriends oozing olive oil,
Do any of your fellow slaves
Have hair a wee bit glossier?
Do I enjoy a salad that's   220
A smidgen tastier? I know,
You don't care very much for oil;
You like to drench yourself in wine.
I'll check your faults in one fell swoop
If my commands aren't all obeyed.][8]
                              (*exit* GYMNASIUM)

But you, who are always on the point
Of paying cash for liberty,   225
So skilled in promising, less skilled
In having promises fulfilled:
Phoenicium, it's you I mean,
You plaything of the upper class!
Unless your boyfriends' grand estates
Provide me all your keep today,
Tomorrow, dear Phoenicium,
I'll tan your hide Phoenician red
And pack you off to the whorehouse shed.
                              (*exit* PHOENICIUM)

Act I, Scene 3

Calid.   Pseudolus, don't you hear what he's saying?   230

Pseud.   Sir, my attention's undivided.

Calid.   Help me: what should I send this man
         To stop my girl from going on sale?

---

[8]The passage in square brackets has been suspected or excluded by a number of scholars;
Ballio's address to Gymnasium seems disproportionately long.

Pseud.	Don't worry! Keep your mind unclouded;
	I'll look after you and me.
	This fellow and I've been friends for years;
	We've traded favors back and forth.
	I'll send him a great big birthday gift:
	A bulging bundle of misery.

Calid.   What's the use?

Pseud.   Can't you change the subject?   235

Calid.   But—

Pseud.   Tut!

Calid.   I'm tortured!

Pseud.   Toughen up!

Calid.   I can't.

Pseud.   Well, force yourself!

Calid.   How can I?

Pseud.   Try to control your emotions, man!
Concentrate on constructive thoughts;
When things go wrong, don't pander to passion.

Calid.   That's all nonsense; there's no pleasure
In love unless you can play the fool.

Pseud.   Must you?

Calid.   Pseudolus, let me be silly. Please!

Pseud.   I'll let you, if you let me leave.

Calid.   Wait! Wait! I'll be just the way you want me.   240

Pseud.   Now you're sounding sensible.

Ballio   It's late; time's wasting. Move, slave, move!
        (BALLIO *and his* SLAVE *start to move offstage.*)

Calid.   Hey, he's leaving. Why not call him?

Pseud.   (*restraining* CALIDORUS) Slow down! Easy does it.

Calid.   He mustn't leave.

Ballio   Dammit, move, you lazy slave!

Pseud.   (*aloud to* BALLIO) Birthday boy! Hey, birthday boy!
        I'm calling you. Hey, birthday boy!
        Come on back, take a look at us.
        Though you're such a busy person,
        We'll detain you. Wait! See,
        People want to talk to you!   245

Ballio   What's this? Who'd hold up
        A very busy man like me?

Pseud.   A friend and helpmate from your past.

Ballio   The past is dead; I live right now.

Pseud.   You blasted boor!

Ballio   You blasted bother!

Calid.   Seize the fellow; chase him!

Ballio   (*to his* SLAVE) Move on, boy.

Pseud.   Let's go round and block his way.   250

Ballio   Jupiter damn you, whoever you are!

Pseud.   I wish you—

Ballio   —the same to you both!
        Come on, forward march, my boy.

Pseud.   May we not have a word with you?

Ballio   No, you may not when I'm not in the mood.

Pseud.   Not even something advantageous?

Ballio   Will you or won't you let me leave?

Pseud.   No, wait!

Ballio   Let go.

Calid.   Ballio, listen! Are you deaf?

Ballio   Yes, to empty words and wallets.   255

Calid.   I always gave you cash in the past.

Ballio   Cash in the past is not what I'm after.

Calid.   I'll give when I get it.

Ballio   You'll have when you've got it.

Calid.   Oh, how foolishly I've wasted
            All my presents and payments to you!

Ballio   Now that your account's defunct
            You want to pay me off in words.
            Stupid boy! Your books are closed.   260

Pseud.   Just realize who this boy is!

Ballio   I've known for ages who he *was*;
            He should discover who he *is*.
            (*to his* SLAVE) Let's get walking.

Pseud.   Ballio, could you
            Grant us just a single glance?
            There may be filthy lucre.

Ballio	*Lucre!*
	That's a word that's worth a glance.
	If I were involved in sacrifice 265
	To mighty Jupiter on high,
	Holding sacred vessels in my hands,
	And there and then I saw a chance
	Of finding filthy lucre—well,
	I'd ditch the whole divine affair.
	All else aside, lucre's one
	Religious force I can't resist.

Pseud. (*to* CALIDORUS) The gods we honor and revere
This fellow holds in total scorn.

Ballio (*aside*) I'll speak to him. (*to* PSEUD.) My kindest greetings,
Most egregious slave in Athens! 270

Pseud. This lad and I would like the gods
To shower blessings on your head;
But, if you get your just deserts,
The gods are bound to cut you dead.

Ballio (*ignoring* PSEUDOLUS) What's the trouble, Calidorus?

Calid. Love and cruel lack of cash.

Ballio "What a pity!" I might say—
If pity kept my stomach full.

Pseud. O.K. We know the type you are:
No need at all to advertise. 275
But do you know what we want?

Ballio Oh, Pollux! Pretty well: trouble for me!

Pseud. That, too; but there is something else.
Come on, pay attention.

Ballio I'm listening.
Since you see I'm very busy,
Keep your story cut and dried.

Pseud.	My man's ashamed, because he promised
	On the appointed day to give you
	Twenty minas for his girl,
	And hasn't arranged delivery.

280

Ballio	If you've got to bear some burden,
	Shame's far easier than disgust.
	He hasn't delivered: he's feeling down;
	I haven't collected: I'm fed up!

Pseud.	He'll come across, he'll raise the money;
	Just you wait a few more days.
	You see, he's terribly afraid
	You'll sell his girl friend out of spite.

| *Ballio* | If he wanted, he had a chance |
| | To pay me the money long ago. |

285

| *Calid.* | What if I didn't have the cash? |

Ballio	If you were in love, you'd have floated a loan.
	You could have gone to a financier;
	You could have carried a carrying charge;
	You could have defrauded dear old Dad.

Pseud.	This boy defraud his dad? Outrageous!
	No danger you would ever suggest
	A moral act!

| *Ballio* | That would be un–pimp–ly. |

Calid.	How could I defraud my father,
	When he's such a sly old man?
	And even if I had the chance,
	Filial love forbids!

290

Ballio	I see.
	Then hug that filial love of yours
	At night instead of Phoenicium.
	But since you apparently prefer
	To put filial love before romance,
	Is every man alive your father?

Is there no one you could ask
To lend you money?

Calid.   Lend? Oh, no:
The word itself is dead and buried.   295

Pseud.   Holy Herc, no lending these days!
Bloated bankers leave the table
Gorged on debts that they've recalled,
And let their creditors go starving;
All the world is far too cagey
Ever to credit another man.

Calid.   I'm most unhappy. I can't find
A solitary silver piece;
And so, unhappily I die
Of love and lack of currency.   300

Ballio   Corner the market in olive oil!
Speculate and sell for cash.
By Herc, I'm sure that you could put
At least two hundred in your pocket.

Calid.   Fat chance! The wretched law declares
I'm underage. Everyone's scared
To give me credit.

Ballio   That's my kind
Of law: I'm scared to give you credit.

Pseud.   Credit! Hey, aren't you satisfied
To know how useful he's been to you?   305

Ballio   There's no such thing as a useful lover
Unless he gives perpetually.
Let him give, give; and when there's
Nothing left, then let him cease to love.

Calid.   Have you no pity?

Ballio   Look: you're coming
Empty-handed. Words don't clink.

                    Yet I sincerely hope you'll live
                    And thrive.

Pseud.   You speak as if he's dying.

Ballio   Dead, as far as I'm concerned—
          If he keeps on talking the way he has.   310
          A lover's given up the ghost
          When he starts pleading with a pimp.
          Learn to sing a loud lament
          That has a silvery, tinkling tune;
          Toward your present woeful dirge
          About your lack of cash, I feel
          A stepmother's sympathy.

Pseud.   What?
          Were you once married to his father?

Ballio   God forbid!

Pseud.   Do as we ask you, Ballio.   315
          Give *me* credit, if you're afraid
          To trust this boy. Within three days
          By land or sea (or somewhere else)
          I'll scrape this money up for you.

Ballio   Give *you* credit?

Pseud.   Why not?

Ballio   Well,
          To give you credit would be much
          Like tying up a hungry dog
          With twisted strips of mutton tripe.

Calid.   How, when I'm so deserving, can you
          Show this kind of gratitude?   320

Ballio   Well, what do you want?

Calid.   I want you to wait,
          Six days only, more or less,

And don't sell her or destroy me,
The man who loves her.

Ballio   Oh, cheer up!
I'm prepared to wait six months.

Calid.   Hurray! You dear, delightful man!

Ballio   Hang on—do you want me to increase
Your happiness a hundredfold?

Calid.   How so?

Ballio   By telling you, right now
Phoenicium is not for sale.   325

Calid.   She isn't?

Ballio   That's a fact, by Herc!

Calid.   (*ecstatically*) Pseudolus, go, get holy victims,
Beasts and butchers; I would pay
This Jove a sacrifice divine.
I now regard our friend right here
As a mightier Jove than Jupiter.

Ballio   No victims, please. I much prefer
To be appeased with chunks of lamb.

Calid.   Hurry! Move! Go get the lambs!
Do you hear what Jupiter has said?   330

Pseud.   I'll soon be back; but first I've got
To run outside the city gate.

Calid.   Why there?

Pseud.   I'll find two human butchers,
Armed with deadly warning bells;[9]

---

[9] Roman public executioners, who did their gruesome work outside the Esquiline Gate, signaled their actions by ringing ominous bells. Pseudolus is suggesting that executioners and floggers will be an appropriate offering for the "god" Ballio.

And while I'm there, I'll bring two flocks
Of weeping-willow flogging whips:
Today there'll be a sweet supply
Of offerings for this Jupiter.

Ballio   Go hang yourself!

Pseud.   No, hanging's what
They do to a pimp-ly Jupiter.   335

Ballio   You wouldn't stand to gain a thing
If I should die.

Pseud.   Why not?

Ballio   Well, look:
If I were dead, in all of Athens
There'd be no one worse than you.

Calid.   Holy Herc, you've got to tell me—
Answer seriously, please: 340
You haven't got my girl for sale,
My lovely, dear Phoenicium?

Ballio   She's not for sale; by Pollux, no.
You see, I sold her long ago.

Calid.   You sold her? How?

Ballio   Right off the stall:
Neck and gizzard, guts and all.

Calid.   You sold my girl?

Ballio   Precisely so;
For twenty minas.

Calid.   Twenty?

Ballio   Yes.
Or four times five, if you prefer.   345

I sold her to a soldier boy,
A captain out of Macedon.
He paid me fifteen in advance.

Calid.   What am I hearing?

Ballio   That your girl's
Converted into currency.

Calid.   How could you?

Ballio   Well, I felt like it;
And she was mine.

Calid.   Ho! Pseudolus:
Run, fetch a sword!

Pseud.   Why do I need
A sword?

Calid.   To kill this man—and me!

Pseud.   Why not just destroy yourself?
This fellow soon will starve to death.   350

Calid.   (*to* BALLIO) What do you say, you ultimate
Extreme of human perjury?
Did you swear that you would never
Sell her to anyone but me?

Ballio   I did, and I admit it.

Calid.   Well, then.
Hadn't you pledged, and formally, too?

Ballio   Yes, but I fudged; I normally do.

Calid.   Perjury! You criminal!

Ballio   I put some money in my pocket.
If that's criminal, don't knock it.   355

147

You've got virtue and family fame—
But not a penny to your name.

Calid.   Pseudolus, stand on the other side
And pile the curses on him.

Pseud.   Fine.
I wouldn't be more keen to run
To the praetor for my liberty.

Calid.   Bring on the insults!

Pseud.   Here we go;
My tongue will tear you limb from limb.
Shameless!

Ballio   All right.

Pseud.   *Criminal!*

Ballio   That's true enough.

Pseud.   *You whipping-boy!*   360

Ballio   Why not?

Pseud.   *Grave-robber!*

Ballio   Certainly.

Pseud.   *Filthy jailbird!*

Ballio   Excellent!

Pseud.   *Treacherous swindler!*

Ballio   That's my style.

Pseud.   *Foul assassin!*

Ballio   Yes. Continue.

Calid.   *Sacrilegious!*

Ballio   I admit it.

Calid.   *Perjurer!*

Ballio   An old refrain.

Calid.   *Lawbreaker!*

Ballio   Most emphatically.

Pseud.   *Youth-corrupter!*

Ballio   Ouch! That stings.

Calid.   *Thief!*

Ballio   Touché!

Pseud.   *Deserter!*

Ballio   Bravo!

Calid.   *Public fraud!*

Ballio   Too obvious.   365

Pseud.   *Crooked cheater!*

Calid.   *Dirty pimp!*

Pseud.   *You crud!*

Ballio   Your voices are divine.

Calid.   *You beat your father and your mother!*

Ballio   And what's more, I killed them both
         Rather than provide them food;
         Was that an awful thing to do?

Pseud.   We're pouring all our juicy words
           In a bottomless pot—a waste of time.

Ballio   Is there nothing else you'd like to say?

Calid.   Are you incapable of shame?   370

Ballio   Or you—a lover who's been found
           As empty as a rotten nut?
           (*reconsidering*) And yet, although you've shouted many
           Nasty noises at my head,
           If that captain doesn't bring
           The other five he owes me still
           By today, the final deadline
           Formally agreed for payment—
           Well, if he can't deliver, then
           I think I can act in character.   375

Calid.   How's that?

Ballio   If *you* bring me the money,
           Then I'll break my word with *him*:
           I'm that kind of character. I'd gladly
           Chat with you, but it's not worthwhile.
           If you're broke, it's a hopeless effort
           Pleading with me to pity you.
           Here's my final word on the subject:
           Focus on the job at hand.

Calid.   You're leaving?

Ballio   I've got many worries
           On my mind.

           (BALLIO *and his* SLAVE *leave for the marketplace, stage left.*)

Pseud.   You'll soon have more!   380
           (*to audience*) I own that fellow now, unless
           All gods and men abandon me.
           I'll bone and fillet him, the way

A cook prepares a slippery eel.
Now, Calidorus, give me your
Attention.

Calid. What is your command?

Pseud. I want this town placed under siege;
I've got to capture it today.
To do that, I'll require a man
Who's wily, clever, cunning, crafty,   385
Able to execute commands,
Not fall asleep when he's on watch.

Calid. What do you intend to do?

Pseud. When the time is ripe, I'll let you know.
I don't want to repeat myself:
That's how plays become too long.

Calid. Very good and very fair.

Pseud. Hurry! Bring him right away.

Calid. Of all our friends, there are so few
A man can really depend upon.   390

Pseud. I know that. You've a double job:
Prepare a prime selection drawn from
All our friends; then pick out one
That we can really count on.

Calid. I'll have him here at once.

Pseud.   Get moving,
Won't you? Talking means delay.

Act I, Scene 4

As CALIDORUS *leaves (stage right) to find an accomplice,* PSEUDOLUS *moves downstage to address the audience.*

Pseud.	He's gone; you're on your own now, Pseudolus.
	Now what'll you do? You've loaded master's son 395
	With precious promises; can you get the goods?
	If you haven't a particle of a proper plan
	You can't begin to weave a cunning cloth
	Or execute a definite design. 400
	But look at the poet: when he starts to write,
	He seeks what doesn't exist, and then he finds it;
	He makes invented fiction look like truth.
	All right, I'll be a poet! Twenty coins,
	Which don't exist on the face of earth, I'll find. 405
	Ages ago I said I'd give him the money,
	Hoping to lay a snare for our old man;
	But somehow "Dad" got wind of what I wanted.

(Simo *and* Callipho *appear from the forum, stage left.*)

	I must control my voice and hold my tongue;
	Look! Here's my master Simo coming this way, 410
	Strolling with his neighbor Callipho.
	Out of this old tomb today I'll dig up
	Twenty coins to give to master's son.
	I'll step aside and hear their conversation.

Act I, Scene 5

Enter the two old men and neighbors, Simo *and* Callipho. Simo, *who is Calidorus' father and Pseudolus' master, is severe in temperament;* Callipho *is more tolerant and urbane.*

Simo	If all the spendthrifts and the lovesick boys 415
	In Athens met to elect a president,
	I'm sure that no one would defeat my son.
	He's the only topic of the town—
	How he wants to free his girl by scrounging
	Money to save her. People tell me this; 420
	In fact, I sniffed the truth a while back
	But pretended not to know.
Pseud.	*(aside)* His son must stink.
	The plot is killed; the whole affair is jammed.

I meant to take this route to silver city;
Now I find the road's completely blocked.   425
He's on to us: no spoils for the despoilers!

Calli.   People who blab or listen to slanderous gossip,
If I were in charge of things, would all be hanged:
Blabbers by the tongue, listeners by the ears.
These stories that they tell you—that your son   430
Is so in love he'd swindle you of silver—
Chances are that these reports are lies.
But even if they're absolutely true,
In the light of present morals, what did he do
Remarkable? What's new if a young man
Loves or frees a mistress?

Pseud.   (aside) Charming fellow!   435

Simo   As an old man I object.

Calli.   But that's no use.
You shouldn't have done these things when you were young.
A father must be pure if he insists
That his son be purer than he's been himself.
When you were young, the damage that you caused   440
Was enough to share with every man alive!
"A chip off the old block": what's the big surprise?

Pseud.   (aside) O Zeus,[10] how few obliging men there are.
Hey! That's the kind of father a son should have.

Simo   Who's talking here? It's my slave Pseudolus.   445
He's the corrupter of my son, the crook!
He's the leader, he's the teacher, he's the one
That I want crucified.

Calli.   Now that's just silly,
Flying off the handle. How much better
To go up and ask him diplomatically   450
Whether those reports are true or false.
When times are tough, good heart is half the battle.

---

[10]Here Pseudolus uses a Greek oath, and will later deliver his oracular responses in Greek. I have decided to avoid any illogical modern bilingualism.

Simo	I'll take your advice.

Pseud. (*aside*) Here they come, Pseudolus.
Prepare your speech to take the old man on.
(*aloud*) Good health to master first, that's only fair;   455
What health is left can be his neighbor's share.

Simo   Good day. What are you doing?

Pseud.   Standing here like this.

Simo   See his attitude, Callipho? King of the roost!

Calli. I think he displays a fine self-confidence.

Pseud. A slave who's free of crime and free of cunning   460
Should stand tall in his master's company.

Calli. We want to question you about some news
That's reached us, sort of drifting through a cloud.

Simo   His words will now convince you that you've taken on
Not Pseudolus, but Socrates.   465

Pseud. All right. I realize you've always put me down;
I know you've got no confidence in me.
You'd like me worthless; still, I'll be first-class.

Simo   Keep your ear space vacant, Pseudolus;
Admit my words as tenants for a while.   470

Pseud. Speak your mind, though I'm furious at you.

Simo   A slave, furious at me, your master?

Pseud.   Does that
Seem so strange?

Simo   Great Herc! According to you,
I've got to guard against your rage. You plan
To batter me the way I batter you.   475
(*to* CALLIPHO) What do you think?

Calli.	I feel his anger's justified,
	When you place no confidence in him.

Simo	All right,
	Let him rage! I'll stop him doing any damage.
	(*to* PSEUDOLUS) Well? What about my question?

Pseud.	Go ahead and ask.
	Treat my knowledge as your Delphic oracle.

480

Simo	Pay attention, then, and remember your promise.
	What do you say? Do you know my son's in love
	With a music-girl?

Pseud. (*in oracular tones*) Yea, yea, forsooth.

Simo And he wants her freed?

Pseud. In truth, forsooth.

Simo	And twenty silver minas,
	Through skulduggery and dirty tricks,
	You're planning to snatch from me?

485

Pseud. I? Snatch from you?

Simo	Yes. To give my son, to free his girl.
	Confess it! Speak: in truth, forsooth?

Pseud. In truth, forsooth.

Simo He admits it! Didn't I tell you, Callipho?

Calli. I remember.

Simo	The moment you knew this, why was it
	Concealed from me? Why didn't I hear?

490

Pseud.	I'll tell you.
	I didn't want to breed a wicked custom
	By denouncing master A to master B.

Simo	This fellow's fit for service in the mill!
Calli.	But Simo, has he sinned?
Simo	You bet he has!

495

Pseud.	Please stop. I keep my own books, Callipho;
	My sins belong to me. Just listen; I'll
	Explain why I shut you out of the love affair.
	I knew I'd land in the gristmill, if I spoke.

Simo	Didn't you know the mill would be your lot
	If you kept mum?

500

Pseud.	I knew.
Simo.	Why wasn't I told?
Pseud.	One fate was instant; one was more remote.
	Silence gained me a day or two of grace.

Simo	What'll you do now? There's no hope of pinching
	Money out of me; I'm wide awake.
	I'll pass a law: "*Don't lend to Pseudolus!*"

505

Pseud.	Ye gods! I'll never beg from another man
	While you're alive. You'll give the cash yourself.
	I'll wheedle it from you.

Simo	From me?
Pseud.	Precisely.
Simo	Holy Herc, knock out my eye, if I give.
Pseud.	You'll give.

510

	Watch out; you've got fair warning.
Calli.	One thing's sure:
	If you succeed, you'll stage a stunning coup!

Pseud.   I will.

Simo   And if you don't?

Pseud.   Then flog me with canes.
         But what if I pull it off?

Simo   So help me Jove,
         You'll live your life unpunished.

Pseud.   Don't forget!   515

Simo   You think I can't take care, when I'm forewarned?

Pseud.   You're warned: take care! You're told: take care! *Take care!*
         Those hands will bestow the cash on me today.

Calli.   He's a living masterpiece if he keeps his word.

Pseud.   Haul me off into slavery if I fail.   520

Simo   Very generous! You're mine already.

Pseud.   Do you want to hear a more amazing story?

Calli.   Gladly! I love to listen to you talk.

Pseud.   (*to* SIMO) Before I tackle you, I'll first engage
         Another foe in a memorable match.   525

Simo   What other foe?

Pseud.   This pimp, your neighbor here.
         Through trickery and dirty double-dealing,
         I'll deprive our precious pandering pimp
         Of the music-girl your son adores.

Simo   You will?

Pseud.   The two campaigns will be finished by this evening.   530

Simo	If you carry out these tasks, as you declare, You'll be mightier than King Agathocles.[11] But if you fail, won't I be justified In sending you to the mill?

Pseud.	Not just for a day, But for all eternity! If I succeed, 535 Will you give me the cash to pay the pimp, Of your own free will?

Calli.	(*to* SIMO) That's reasonable and fair; Say yes.

Simo	But something's just occurred to me. What if there's collusion, Callipho, Or they've arranged some underhanded deal 540 To dupe me of my wealth?

Pseud.	Not even I Would have the nerve to stoop so low! Look here: If there's collusion, Simo, or if we Have ever wheeled and dealed in such a way, Then use your whip like a writing instrument And scratch red letters all across my back. 545

Simo	Your comedy can start now, any time.

Pseud.	Help me out today, please, Callipho; Don't get involved in any other scheme.

Calli.	I had set up a visit to the country.

Pseud.	Un-set it then; upset your settled plans. 550

Calli.	All right, I'll choose to stay on your account; I yearn to watch you in action, Pseudolus. And if I see him holding back the cash He promised, I'll come through with it myself.

---

[11] Agathocles had been a famous tyrant and king of Syracuse about a hundred years earlier (317–289 B.C.).

Simo	I won't renege.

Pseud.   By Pollux, if you do,   555
You'll be dunned to death with a devastating din.
Come on now, move along inside, you two,
And give my tricks some room: it's their turn now.

Calli.   All right; you'll get your way.

Pseud.   Remember, don't
Leave home today.

Calli.   I promise you my help.   560
           (CALLIPHO *enters his house.*)

Simo   Well, I'm off to the forum. I'll be back here.

Pseud.   Make it soon! (*exit* SIMO, *stage left*)

(PSEUDOLUS *moves downstage again to address the audience.*)
I suspect that you're suspicious of me now.
You think I'm making these grand promises
To entertain you, till our play is done.
You don't expect me to do what I said I would.   565
Well, I won't back down. One fact I know for sure:
I don't quite know just how I'll pull it off . . .
And yet I'll manage! Somehow every actor ought
To bring some novel innovation to the stage.
If he can't, he should give way to one who can.   570

I think I'll step inside here for a while
To drill my regiment of roguery.

I'll hurry back; expect a brief delay.
Here's music that will charm the time away.
                  (*exit into house*)

ACT II

A very short time has elapsed. PSEUDOLUS *emerges from Simo's house, in obvious good spirits.*

Act II, Scene 1

Pseud. Great Jupiter! How sweet to find
       That everything is working out!
       I've chased anxiety and doubt
       From this grand scheme I have in mind.   575
       It's stupid to entrust a plan
       To a weak or wishy-washy man;
       For all endeavors must depend
       On how much effort you expend.

       Inside my brain I've so prepared
       My tricky troops, my sneaky squad   580
       Of flimflam, fakery, and fraud,
       That, after war has been declared,
       My ancestral fortitude, combined
       With hard work and a nasty mind,
       Will snare my enemies with ease,
       And falsely force them to their knees.

       This adversary that I share
       With all you lusty men out there,
       This Ballio I'll bash and break:
       Just pay attention, for my sake.   585

       Today I will besiege this town,
       Draw up my legions, tear it down;
       And when I've stormed and scaled that wall

(My men won't find it hard at all),
I'll lead my army straightaway
To a second town, all old and gray.
This will provide my friends and me
With loads of booty, duty-free.
My destiny, the world will know,
Is striking panic in the foe.
It's in my blood: I feel the need
To carry out some doughty deed—   590
A hero's act, enshrined in fame,
That will perpetuate my name.

But who's this fellow striding up?
   He's quite unknown to me;
And why's he coming with that sword?
   I'll step aside and see.

Act II, Scene 2

From the harbor (stage right) there appears a figure dressed in the conventional traveler's outfit of cloak, broad-brimmed hat, and conspicuous sword. It is HARPAX, *the somewhat dim-witted messenger slave of the Macedonian captain.*

Harpax   Here we are, the neighborhood
My master carefully described.   595
Everything seems to correspond
With my instructions from the captain:
Seventh block beyond the gate,
The home of Ballio the pimp,
The fellow I'm supposed to give
This token and this moneybag.
But I could use some guidance now.
Which one's the pimp's establishment?

Pseud.   (*aside*) Quiet! Shh! I've got this man,
If heaven and earth approve my plan.   600
But I'll require a new invention:
Here's a sudden, new dimension.
Let's proceed with all dispatch;
Scrap the old scheme, start from scratch!

> I'll pulverize and quite destroy
> This regimental errand-boy.

Harpax   I'll knock on the door and see if I
Can rouse up anyone inside.
(*He knocks loudly on Ballio's door.*)

Pseud.   (*rushing up to* HARPAX) Knock it off, whoever you are;   605
Please save your knocks and spare these doors.
I'm here to plead on their behalf
As guardian patron of the portals.

Harpax   Are you Ballio?

Pseud.   Not quite,
But I'm Assistant Ballio.

Harpax   What's that supposed to mean?

Pseud.   It means
I'm Exchequer, In-checker, Prince of the Pantry.

Harpax   Sort of majordomo?

Pseud.   Higher up
In rank: I'm General Factotum.

Harpax   What's your status, slave or free?

Pseud.   Right at the moment, I'm a slave.   610

Harpax   You look the part. You don't appear
A candidate for liberty.

Pseud.   Shouldn't you check the looking glass
When you've got insults to unload?

Harpax   (*aside*) This fellow's just a troublemaker.

Pseud.   (*aside*) Gods be gracious, here's an anvil
For my craft! I'll hammer out
A brazen masterpiece today.

Harpax	*(aside)* Why's he talking to himself?

Pseud.   Look here, you youngster!

Harpax   What do you want?   615

Pseud.   Do you or don't you represent
That Macedonian officer
Who bought a beauty from our stock,
Who paid my master, Mister Pimp,
A cash advance of fifteen minas,
Five still owing?

Harpax   I'm your man.
But how in the world do you know me?
Where have you seen or talked to me?
I've never made a trip to Athens   620
In the past, and till today,
I'd never laid an eye on you.

Pseud.   It's just because you look the part.
When he left town, we all agreed
The balance would fall due today,
But no cold comfort has arrived.

Harpax   Well, here it is.

Pseud.   You've brought it?

Harpax   Yes.

Pseud.   Then why so slow to hand it over?   625

Harpax   Give it to you?

Pseud.   Yes, Herc, to me!
I'm Ballio's financial wizard:
Bursar, purser, debt–disperser.

Harpax   Holy Herc, if you controlled
The treasure of almighty Jove,

I'd never trust you with a single
Silver sliver!

Pseud.   (*reaching for the bag*) Quick as a wink
We'll see your debt discharged.

Harpax   (*protecting the bag*)
I'd rather keep these funds tied up.   630

Pseud.   Damn you! It's very obvious
You're smearing my integrity—
As though I'd never handled trust
Accounts a thousand times as large.

Harpax   Well, maybe others have more faith;
You don't inspire my confidence.

Pseud.   Are you suggesting I might want
To con the silver out of you?

Harpax   No. You're the source of that suggestion;
My suspicions are my own.   635
But what's your name?

Pseud.   (*aside*) This pimp has a slave called Syrus.
I'll pretend that's me. (*aloud*) I'm Syrus.

Harpax   Syrus?

Pseud.   Yessir, that's my name.

Harpax   We're wasting time. If your master's home,
Why don't you call him to the door,
So I can get my business finished
Here, whatever your name may be.

Pseud.   If he were home, I'd summon him.
But trusting me with all the cash   640
Would be a more conclusive act
Than paying him.

Harpax   Conclusive? Sure!

I'd close the deal and kiss it sweet
Goodbye! Of course, I realize
You're hot and bothered when you see
The money slipping through your claws.
I won't negotiate with anyone
But Ballio in person.

Pseud.   He's occupied and busy now:
He's got a case before the judge.   645

Harpax   Good luck to him! I'll just return
Another time, when he's at home.
But take this letter from me, please,
And give it to him. Inside he'll find
The token our masters both agreed
To use in dealing with the girl.

Pseud.   I understand. Your captain wanted
Her released to anyone
Who brought the cash, together with
His portrait image, stamped in wax.   650
He left a specimen with us.

Harpax   You know about the whole affair.

Pseud.   Why shouldn't I?

Harpax   Then give him the token.

Pseud.   O.K. But what's your name?

Harpax   Harpax.[12]

Pseud.   Harp off, Harpax! You're not welcome.
You won't get inside our house
To play your snatching harpy acts.

Harpax   I snatch great foes right off the battlefield: 655
That's how I got my name.

---

[12]One of Plautus' significant character names, "Harpax" suggests the Greek verb *harpazein,*
"to snatch" or "to plunder."

Pseudolus

| Pseud. | I'm more inclined to think
You snatch great pots right off the pantry shelf. |

Pseud. I'm more inclined to think
You snatch great pots right off the pantry shelf.

Harpax Not true! But Syrus, do you know
What I would like?

Pseud.   I'll know if you tell me.

Harpax I've got a room beyond the gate,
The third tavern on the right;
My hostess is a tubby, chubby,
Gimpy grandma, name of Chrysis.

Pseud. What do you want from me?

Harpax Please reach me there, when your master comes.   660

Pseud. As you would have it, certainly.

Harpax I'm now so weary from my travels,
I must rest and freshen up.

Pseud. A wise and admirable plan.
But please make sure you don't go missing
When I need to summon you.

Harpax No fear. I'll have a delicious meal,
And then an after-dinner nap.

Pseud. I quite approve.

Harpax   And is that all?

Pseud. Go off to slumberland.

Harpax   I'm going.   665
                    (*exit* HARPAX, *stage right*)

Pseud. Just you listen, Harpy-boy:
Bundle up in lots of blankets;
Sweating makes a person sweet.

Act II, Scene 3

Pseud.   (*moving downstage to confide in the audience*)
Immortal gods! I think this fellow
Saved my skin by coming here.
He's paid the ticket for my trip
From Way-off-course to Journey's-end.
Father Nick-of-Time himself
Couldn't have made a timelier entrance
Than this timeliest of letters
That has landed in my lap.   670

Here I've found my horn of plenty—
Plenty of everything I need:
A horn of hoax and hocus-pocus,
Sleight of hand, bamboozlement;
Plenty of cash, and a horny girl
To hug my master's horny son.

How I'm going to swagger now,
When I've got cause for confidence!
Already I'd laid out a plan
Of action, scheming how to snatch
The little lady from the pimp;   675
It all took shape inside my mind,
Well ordered, beautifully arranged.

But this will often be the case:
The plans of a hundred clever men
Can be overturned by a single goddess—
Luck. And isn't it the truth?
Depending on how a person uses Luck
He may succeed, and everyone of course
Will then pronounce him sensible and wise.   680
If a scheme should turn out well, then all the world
Declares him shrewd; but if disaster strikes,
We look upon him as an utter fool.

Well, we're the fools; we just can't see our folly!
All of us pursue our greedy goals,
Grasping at gain, as if we possibly

Could judge what serves our real interest.
We sacrifice the real world
By chasing unreality.
The outcome is predictable: 685
We groan and moan our lives away,
While death creeps closer all the while.

Enough profound philosophy!
My lectures always last too long.

Immortal gods! My little fib
Was worth its weight in platinum—
That sudden, spur-of-the-moment claim
That I belonged to Ballio.
Now I'll use this letter here   690
To dupe three victims: master, pimp,
And military messenger.

What's this? Oh bliss! I think another
Wish I made is coming true.
Look: Calidorus is approaching,
Leading someone by the hand.

Act II, Scene 4

As PSEUDOLUS *steps aside to watch and listen,* CALIDORUS *returns (stage right) with* CHARINUS, *a bright and appealing youth of about his own age.*

Calid.   Sweet and bitter, I've revealed
         The truth in its entirety.
         You know my passion and my pain;
         You know my abject poverty.   695

Chari.   I remember everything;
         Just let me know what I should do.

Calid.   Pseudolus commanded me
         To find a strong and sympathetic
         Friend, and then to bring him here.

Chari.   You've followed orders to the letter:

Here's a friend and sympathy.
But that man Pseudolus of yours
Is new to me.

Calid.　　　　　A living masterpiece!
He's my inventive genius.　　　　　　　　　　700
He told me he could carry out
The project I discussed with you.

Pseud.　(*aside*) I'll try the grand, heroic style.

Calid.　Is that a voice?

Pseud.　　　　　Oh yea, rejoice!
Dire despot, unto thee I bow;
Pseudolus' sovereign lord art thou.
A threefold pleasure, thrice prepared,
Three victims cunningly ensnared
Thou shalt possess: a triple treat;　　　　　705
A triform triumph of deceit.
Judge not this letter by its size:
It holds a vast and precious prize.

Calid.　That's him.

Chari.　　　　　A bold, bombastic beggar!

Pseud.　Forward march, extend your arm,
And greet the answer to your prayer.

Calid.　Pray, how should I greet you, Pseudolus?
As Wishful Hope or Wish Fulfilled?

Pseud.　As both, I'd say.

Calid.　　　　　As both, good day!
But what's the news?

Pseud.　　　　　　Dispel your fear!　　　　　710

Calid.　(*identifying* CHARINUS *for* PSEUDOLUS)
I packed this man out.

169

Pseud.   Come again?

Calid.   I picked him out, I meant to say.

Pseud.   Who is he?

Calid.   Charinus.

Pseud.   Gracious me!
A graceful name! My gratitude.

Chari.   Look, if I can be of service,
Say the word.

Pseud.   Thanks just the same.
Bless you, Charinus, I don't want
The two of us to bother you.

Chari.   Could you two be a bother? Nothing
Bothers me.

Pseud.   Then wait a while.   715

Calid.   What's that you've got?

Pseud.   A letter
I waylaid just now; a token, too.

Calid.   A token? What do you mean, a token?

Pseud.   One the captain sent this way.
His flunky was delivering it,
Along with five bright silver coins;
He'd come to fetch your ladylove,
But I threw dust into his eyes.

Calid.   How?

Pseud.   This audience has paid
To see us act our comedy.   720
They know precisely how it happened;
You'll get caught up later on.

170

Calid. What's our next move?

Pseud.   Today your girl
        Will be free to take you in her arms.

Calid. Me?

Pseud.   Yes you, yourself, in person,
        If yours truly lives so long;
        And if you can find a man to help me—
        Quickly!

Chari.   What should he be like?

Pseud. Immoral, clever, cunning, one
        Who quickly gets the hang of things   725
        And then relies on native wit
        To see what action he should take.
        Someone unknown in these parts.

Chari. If he's a slave, could that create
        A problem?

Pseud.   Not at all; I much
        Prefer the slave to the freeborn.

Chari. Well, I think I can provide your man:
        Quick-witted, rotten to the core.
        My father sent him from Carystus;
        So far, he hasn't ventured from   730
        Our house, and never until yesterday
        Had he set foot in Athens.

Pseud. Wonderful! But I'll still need
        To float a loan—five silver minas,
        Which I'll pay back today; you see,
        His father (*pointing to* CALIDORUS) owes a debt to me.

Chari. I'll lend you the money; look no farther.

Pseud. What a dear, obliging man!

> I'll also need a cloak, a dagger,
> And a broad-brimmed hat.

Chari.   Can do.   735

Pseud.   Immortal gods! This fellow's not
Charinus, he's sweet Charity!
Tell me about your father's slave:
Has he any sense about him?

Chari.   Armpit scents: he stinks to heaven.

Pseud.   Phew! We'll get him longer sleeves.
Can he be sanguine, sharp, and keen?

Chari.   His blood is two parts vinegar.

Pseud.   But what if he has to tap his veins
For sweeter fluids?

Chari.   Sweeter? He'll drip   740
Spiced liqueur and raisin brandy,
Muscatel and honey-mead;
In fact, he had a notion once
To start a walking winery.

Pseud.   Touché, Charinus! You're a treat;
You fleece me at my favorite game.
But how shall I address your flunky?

Chari.   Simia, alias Mister Monkey.

Pseud.   When it's windy, can he whirl?

Chari.   He'd teach a twister how to twirl.   745

Pseud.   Is he cautious?

Chari.   Maybe not:
He's often cautioned, never caught.

Pseud.   What if they nail him fast and firm?

Chari.	He's just an eel: away he'll squirm.
Pseud.	And is he sharp at dirty tricks?
Chari.	Sharp enough for politics.
Pseud.	The man's an ideal choice, to judge From your account.

Chari.   If you only knew!
He'll glance at you, and straightaway
He'll tell you what you want him for.   750
But what's your proposal?

Pseud.   I'll explain.
When I have got him all dressed up,
I want this fellow to become
A counterfeit of the captain's slave;
He'll take the token to the pimp,
Along with the sack of silver coins,
Then whisk the woman off to safety.

Help! I've given the plot away!

Any instructions that remain
I'll tell the fellow face to face.   755

Calid. Then what are we doing standing here?

Pseud. Get the man and all the trappings,
Bring him right away to meet me
At the countinghouse of Aeschinus.
Be quick about it!

Calid.   We'll be there
Ahead of you.
              (*exeunt* CALIDORUS *and* CHARINUS, *stage left*)

Pseud.   More haste, less speed!
(*addressing the audience*)
All my plans that earlier
Were clouded and obscure have now

Become transparent, and my vision's
Crystal clear. The road's wide open: 760
All my legions now are marshaled,
Standards proudly raised on high.
The birds are soaring overhead;
The auspices all point my way.
My heart's abrim with confidence
That I can rout the enemy.
Off to the forum, where I'll load
My orders on this Simia:

He mustn't trip, his leadership
Is crucial in my grand design;   765
I'll sound the call, we'll storm the wall,
And then Fort Pimp will all be mine.

                                        (*exit stage left*)

ACT III

From Ballio's doorway there emerges a YOUNG SLAVE, *a wretched and timid boy in his early teens.*[13]

Act III, Scene 1

Slave   When the gods assign a boy the job of slaving
For a pimp, and then they grant him ugliness,
That boy has been assigned, if you ask me,
A lousy load, a low-down dirty deal.   770
Just look at me slaving here, where I'm obliged
To shore up every shape and size of misery;
And I can't find a single lover-boy
To give me even a smidgen of tenderness.

Today's the birthday of our boss the pimp;   775
He's threatened the household, high and low alike:
Whoever fails to give him a gift today
Will die tomorrow in cruel agony.
Hey! I don't know what I'm supposed to do;
I lack the wherewithal all do it with.   780
If I don't find a present for our pimp,
I'm bound to get the long end of the stick.
That's awful for a little kid like me!

Gosh! I'm so scared of catching holy heck
That if some fellow lays a load on me,   785
Though people say that really makes you groan,
I guess I'll somehow learn to clench my teeth.

I'd better learn to clench my lips. Just look!
My master's coming home; he's brought a cook.

---

[13]On this little monologue, with its sometimes cryptic brand of humor, see General Introduction, note 3.

175

Pseudolus

Act III, Scene 2

As the SLAVE BOY *tries to become invisible, enter (stage left)* BALLIO *and a* COOK, *accompanied by apprentice cooks and other* ATTENDANTS.

Ballio   "Cook's Marketplace"—that's such a stupid name: 790
Not cooks but crooks go on the market there.
Upon my oath, I couldn't hope to find
A worse type than this cook I've got in tow—
A loud-mouthed, swaggering, useless nincompoop.

The King of Hell refused to let him in: 795
He's needed here to cater to the dead,
Since he alone can satisfy their taste.

Cook   If you hold that opinion of me,
Why did you hire me?

Ballio   Scarcity: no choice!
If you're a cook, why were you sitting there,   800
Left out in the market all alone?

Cook   I'll tell you:
Human greed's the cause of my decline,
Not lack of talent.

Ballio   How so?

Cook   Let me explain:
As soon as people come to hire a cook,
Nobody wants the best and highest priced;   805
They'd rather hire the cheapest one around.
That's why I sat alone in the marketplace.
No drachma-per-diem dope am I; no one
Gets me off my butt for less than double that.

My dinner menu's not like other cooks',   810
Who spice up mounds of mouldy meadow grass,
Converting guests to cattle (greens galore!),
Then lace that fodder with more foliage.
They toss in coriander, fennel, garlic,

176

	Parsley, sorrel, cabbage, spinach, beet,	815
	Dissolve a pound of asafetida,	
	Then grind in murderous mustard, guaranteed	
	To make you howl before you touch the stuff.	
	When these boys cook, their seasonings do not	
	Consist of spices, but of vampire bats,	820
	To gnaw the living entrails from their guests.	
	So that's why people here live such short lives,	
	Their bellies bloated with this kind of fodder,	
	Scary to mention, let alone to munch on.	
	Humans choose the greens that cows refuse.	825

Ballio   And you? Do you use heavenly seasoning
That can extend the span of human life,
Since you attack those spices?

Cook   Shout it aloud!
People can aspire to live two hundred years
By sticking to the spicy diets I've designed.   830
When I've put scorchilender in the pan,
Or torridopsis or inflammagon,
The dish becomes red hot upon the spot.
Those are my seasonings for Neptune's creatures;
Earth-born beasts I spice with yummiander,   835
Smackalyptus, or delectamom.

Ballio   May Jupiter and all the gods destroy you
With your spices and your pack of lies!

Cook   Please let me speak.

Ballio   Speak on, and go to hell!

Cook   When the pans are boiling, I remove their lids: 840
The savor flies to heaven on soaring feet.

Ballio   A savor with sore feet?

Cook   A careless slip.

Ballio   How so?

Cook	I meant to say, "on soaring wings."[14] Jupiter dines daily on that scent.	
Ballio	On your day off, what's Jupiter to eat?	845
Cook	He goes to bed on an empty stomach.	
Ballio	Damn you! Is it for this I'm shelling out hard cash?	
Cook	Though I admit I'm an expensive cook, I promise that my hiring price is matched By service rendered.	
Ballio	Larceny, no doubt.	850
Cook	Do you expect to find a single cook Who's not equipped with grasping eagle talons?	
Ballio	Do you expect to cook a single meal Without those grasping talons tightly tied? (*catching sight of the lurking* SLAVE BOY) Hey, boy, look lively! Here's a job for you! Get all my valuables locked away. Don't let this fellow's face out of your sight: If he looks sideways, you look sideways, too. If he steps forward, match him step for step. If he sticks out his hand, you do the same. If he should grab what's his, just let him grab it; But if he grabs what's mine, then hold him fast. He starts: you start. He stops: you stop likewise. He squats upon the ground: just squat away! And each apprentice cook gets a private guard.	855 860 865
Cook	Come on, cheer up!	
Ballio	Will you explain how I Can be cheerful when I'm going home with you?	

---

[14]I have paraphrased Plautus' joke, which is obscure in the original Latin. It is one of his recurrent slip-of-the-tongue gags (cf. *Miles Gloriosus*, line 27).

Cook	Because today I'll dip you in my broth
	The way Medea cooked old Pelias.
	Her poisons and her magic drugs, they tell us,
	Made the old man a little lad again;
	I'll do the same for you.

870

Ballio	So you're also a poisoner?

Cook	Heavens, no! I'm a man-preserver.

Ballio	Ha!
	How much to teach me that single recipe?

875

Cook	Which one?

Ballio	Preserving you from fleecing me.

Cook	Base price, if you trust me; otherwise, no deal.
	But is it your friends or enemies you're going
	To feast today?

Ballio	Why, they're my friends, of course.

Cook	Why don't you call your enemies instead?
	Today I'll give your guests a banquet so bespiced,
	So sprinkled with sweet seasoning,
	The instant someone samples my delights
	He'll want to nibble off his fingertips.

880

Ballio	By Herc, before you serve a single guest,
	Be sure that you and your henchmen have a taste,
	To make you nibble off your pilfering paws.

885

Cook	Perhaps you don't believe what I'm telling you.

Ballio	Don't be a nuisance! Too much nagging! Shush!
	Look: here's my house. Go in and cook your meal.
	Hurry!

890

Slave	Why not sit down and call your guests?
	The dinner's already a mess.

(*The* COOK *and his retinue go into Ballio's house, leaving* BALLIO *alone on stage.*)

Ballio   Just look at the sprig!
That rascal is the cook's assistant tongue.[15]
Really, I don't know where to watch out first,
With thieves inside my house and a thug next door.   895
You see, my neighbor here (Calidorus' dad),
As he left for the forum, warned me specially
To be on guard against Pseudolus, his slave,
And not to trust him; for he's on the prowl today,
Hoping somehow to swindle the girl from me.   900
The old man said he'd promised solemnly
That he would filch away Phoenicium.

So now I'll go inside and tell my household staff
On no account to trust this Pseudolus riffraff.
                       (*goes into his house*)

---

[15] The "rascal" must be the slave who has just spoken in lines 891–92. This person could be either the young slave of Act III, Scene 1 (if he is still on stage), or an impudent assistant cook.

ACT IV

PSEUDOLUS *enters from the forum (stage left), singing exultantly to his newly found assistant, the slave* SIMIA. SIMIA, *who does not appear immediately, is disguised as the messenger-slave Harpax, with cloak, broad hat, and conspicuous sword; in guile and virtuosity, he can rival Pseudolus.*

Act IV, Scene 1

Pseud.   If ever immortal benevolent gods
    Get involved in our human condition,   905
They must want Calidorus and me to be saved,
    And the pimp to go down to perdition.
What a godsent support they've provided in you:
    You're a fellow so cunning and clever!
(*looking back, and failing to see* SIMIA)
Where's he gone? If I've started to talk to myself,
    I'm becoming more loony than ever.

    By Herc, I'm tricked, it's plain to see:
    I failed to check a cheat like me.

Holy Pollux, I'm ruined if he's taken off,
    My design won't unfold as expected.   910
Look at that! There's my whipping-post strutting along,
    With his arrogant manner perfected.
(*to* SIMIA) Hello, there, I was hunting all over for you;
    I was frightened that you had defected.

Simia   I confess I'm a frightfully flighty type.

Pseud.   Where were you dawdling?

Simia   Wherever I pleased.

Pseud.	I know that already.
Simia	Then why do you ask?
Pseud.	I want to school you in this scheme.
Simia	You need the school; don't scholar me.

915

Pseud.	You're treating me with cool contempt.
Simia	Don't you deserve contempt from me, A legendary legionary?
Pseud.	Concentrate on the job at hand.
Simia	Do you see my attention wandering?
Pseud.	Then walk along more quickly.
Simia	No, I like to take my time.

920

Pseud.	Here's our chance: while he's asleep, I want you to get the jump on him.
Simia	Why such a rush? Relax! No fear! If only Jupiter would place That soldier's emissary here To meet my challenge, face to face: There's no way he could ever be A Harpax half as good as me.

925

	Cheer up! I'll fix your fine affair, Untangling it with tender care. My tricks and lies will so dismay This foreign army type, he'll say He isn't who he seems to be; He'll calmly claim that I am he.
Pseud.	How come?

930

Simia	How dumb a question! I'm going to die!

Pseud.   (*aside*) A really charming sort of guy!

Simia   I'll outclass even you in lying,
Master snitch, without half trying.

Pseud.   Jupiter watch over you
For my sake!

Simia   And for my sake, too.
Does this outfit suit me, would you say?   935

Pseud.   It's quite magnificent!

Simia   O.K.

Pseud.   I pray the kindly gods may grant you
Everything for which you yearn;
If I prayed them to grant what you were worth,
You'd get less than nothing in return.
(*aside*) He's so downright sly and sneaky;
I've never seen a man more cheeky.

Simia   What's that I heard?

Pseud.   Hey, mum's the word.
But what rewards you'll get from me
If you manage this business properly!

Simia   Won't you shut up?
Reminding the mindful is mindless and mad: 940
The rememberer's memory may become bad.
I've absorbed all the facts and I've learned them by heart;
I've religiously practiced my fraudulent part.

Pseud.   An upright man!

Simia   (*aside*) Not he nor I.

Pseud.   Don't falter now!

Simia   Won't you shut up?

Pseud.   So help me heaven—

Simia   But heaven won't;
            You're spouting undiluted lies.

Pseud.   For your treachery, Simia, you have earned
            My love, my fear, my high esteem.

Simia   I've learned to hand out guff like that;
            You can't pat me upon the head.   945

Pseud.   What a lovely reception you'll get from me
            When you've done this job today!

Simia   Ha, ha!

Pseud.   With lovely food and wine and perfume,
            Succulent morsels and drinks galore.
            A lovely girl will be there as well,
            To lavish kisses upon you.

Simia   You're a lovely host.

Pseud.   I'll cause you to say
            Much more, if you pull off this job.

Simia   If I don't, may the crucifixioner
            Give me a cross reception!   950
            Now get a move on! Show me the mouth
            Of the pimp's establishment. Which door?

Pseud.   Third along here.

Simia   Shh! That mouth just
            Yawned.

Pseud.   The house has a bellyache,
            I'd say.

Simia   Why?

Pseud.   Because, so help me
Pollux, it's vomiting the pimp!

(PSEUDOLUS *and* SIMIA *make themselves inconspicuous, as* BALLIO *emerges from his house in an odd, furtive manner.*)

Simia   Is that the man?

Pseud.   That's him.

Simia   What measly
Merchandise! Just take a look:
Forward motion's not for him;
He skitters sideways like a crab.   955

Act IV, Scene 2

Ballio   I'll admit this cook's less foul
A character than I supposed;
So far he's pilfered nothing but
A ladle and a little mug.

Pseud.   (*to* SIMIA, *sotto voce*)
Here you go now, this is the perfect
Moment.

Simia   I agree with you.

Pseud.   Step out into the street. Be tricky!
I'll be waiting in ambush here.

Simia   (*in a loud "soliloquy," moving toward* BALLIO)
I've been counting carefully:
Sixth lane from the city gate.   960
Here we are; this must be the alley
Where he told me to turn aside.
But how many houses down the alley,
That I really couldn't say.

Ballio	(*aside*) Who's this fellow in the cloak?
	Where's he come from? Who does he want?
	He's got a sort of foreign look, and
	I don't recognize his face.

Simia	Here's a man who's sure to know	
	The matter I'm unsure about.	965

Ballio	(*aside*) He's heading straight for me. I wonder
	Where in the world the fellow's from.

Simia	Hey there! You with the wild goatee,
	I've got a question; answer me.

Ballio	Well, well! You've no "good day" to share?

Simia	No, I have no good days to spare.

Ballio	You'll get from me as good as you give.

Pseud.	(*aside*) A fine beginning: superlative!	970

Simia	Tell me, then, do you know any
	Person living on this lane?

Ballio	I know myself.

Simia	Few human beings
	Reach the condition you describe.
	Down in the forum I doubt you'd find
	One man in ten who knows himself.

Pseud.	(*aside*) I'm safe; he's turned philosopher.

Simia	I'm looking for a nasty fellow—
	Scofflaw, low-life, perjurer,
	Degenerate.

Ballio	(*aside*) It's me he wants.	975
	Those are my nicknames, sure enough.	

I hope he gets my surname right.
(*aloud*) What is this fellow's name?

Simia Pimp Ballio.

Ballio   Do I know myself?
I am the object of your search,
Young man.

Simia   You're Ballio?

Ballio Me, yours truly.

Simia   The way you're dressed,
You look like a second-story man.   980

Ballio If you spotted me on some dark street,
I think you'd treat me with respect.

Simia My master asked me to express
His warmest compliments to you.
Take this letter from me now;
He told me to deliver it.

Ballio Just who issued the command?

Pseud. (*aside*) We're sunk! My man is all mucked up.
Names weren't mentioned; what a mess!

Ballio Who do you say sent me this letter?   985

Simia Look at his picture on the seal;
Then, sir, *you* tell *me* his name,
Proving to me that you are really
Ballio.

Ballio   Give me the letter.

Simia (*handing it over*) Here: identify the seal.

Ballio	(*aside, as he studies the seal*) Ah! Polymachaeroplagides:[16] Pure and simple recognition. (*to* SIMIA) Hey! Polymachaeroplagides Is his name.
Simia	Now I know how right I was in giving you the letter, 990 Seeing how you spoke the name Of Polymachaeroplagides.
Ballio	What's he doing?
Simia	Playing the role Of brave heroic warrior. But hurry up and scrutinize This letter, please—I'm very rushed— Take the cash immediately And give the woman her release. I must be in Sicyon today Or else tomorrow I die. 995 Master's very domineering.
Ballio	Don't tell me; I know him too.
Simia	Come on, read the letter through, then.
Ballio	Well, I will, if you'll shut up. (*reads*) "Captain Polymachaeroplagides Dispatches to the pimp named Ballio This letter sealed with a portrait mutually 1000 Agreed upon."
Simia	The token's in the letter.
Ballio	I see; I'm satisfied. But does he never Start a letter with a friendly wish?

---

[16] A typical bit of comic nonsense, the Greek name means "Son-of-many-sword-blows"; Willcock (p. 129) suggests "McWhackem."

Simia	No; that would violate army protocol.
	By action he confers good health on friends
	And likewise deals destruction to his foes. 1005
	But keep on reading, let experience teach you
	What this letter says.

Ballio　　　　　　　　　Just listen, then:
　　　　"Harpax, my aide, is on his way to you—"
You're Harpax?

Simia　　　　　　　　　I'm your man, (*aside*) and harp I can.   1010

Ballio　"—Bearing this letter. He'll convey the cash;
　　I want the woman sent with him at once.
　　It's right to wish the righteous 'Best of health':
　　I'd do so, if I thought you qualified."

Simia　What next?

Ballio　　　　　　　Pay up and take away the girl.   1015

Simia　What are we waiting for?

Ballio　　　　　　　　　　Follow inside, then.

Simia　　　　　　　　　　　　　　Here I come.

Act IV, Scene 3

As BALLIO *and* SIMIA *disappear into Ballio's house,* PSEUDOLUS *comes down-stage to address the audience yet again.*

Pseud.　I swear to Pollux I've never seen a man
　　More devious or deceitful than this Simia.
　　I'm frightened of the fellow. I'm really scared
　　I'll face the gory treatment Ballio got: 1020
　　My man may turn his lucky horns on me,
　　If any chance of mischief should arise.
　　Heavens! I hope not, for I wish him well.

Now I'm feeling triply terrified.
First, I'm nervous that my pal here could   1025
Desert me and defect to the enemy;
Next, master might arrive back anytime,
To snatch the loot and catch the looters, too;
Finally, Harpax the First could reappear   1030
Before this Harpax gets the girl away.

Oh Herc, I'm doomed! They've been inside too long.
My heart is waiting with its suitcase packed;
It plans to fly away to distant realms,
Unless he brings the girl out right away.   1035

(*seeing Ballio's door open*)
I've won! I've overthrown my overseers!

Act IV, Scene 4

SIMIA *reappears from Ballio's house, leading the girl* PHOENICIUM.

Simia   Don't cry, you don't understand, Phoenicium.
        You'll get the picture soon, at dinner time.
        You're not being led to the fellow with the fangs,   1040
        That Macedonian who provokes your tears;
        I'm taking you to your dearest sweet desire:
        In a twinkling you'll be in Calidorus' arms.

Pseud. Why did you loiter so long inside the house?
        My heart's been battered, bruised, and beaten flat.   1045

Simia   You jailbird, how can you find the luxury
        Of grilling me when the enemy's everywhere?
        I'd say, "Forward march, in double time!"

Pseud. By Pollux, good advice from such a no-good thug!   1050
        Advance! Let's crown our win with a triumphant jug!
                (*They leave with* PHOENICIUM, *stage right.*)[17]

---

[17]Although there is no textual evidence of their destination, it makes good sense to assume that they have taken refuge with Charinus, Calidorus' generous friend from Act II. See Willcock, p. 16.

Act IV, Scene 5

BALLIO *comes out of his house, obviously pleased at the success of his transaction.*

Ballio   Ha, ha! At last my mind's been set at rest:
That fellow's gone; he's led the girl away.
Let Pseudolus come now, the dirty crook,
And try to snatch the girl by trickery!   1055
By Herc, I'm positive I'd rather swear
An oath, commit a thousand perjuries,
Than let that swindler get the laugh on me.
Now when we meet, he'll be my laughingstock.
He's bound for the gristmill soon—that was the deal.   1060

I'd love to meet old Simo, I confess;
How happily he'd share my happiness!

Act IV, Scene 6

SIMO *enters from the forum, stage left.*

Simo   I'll see if my Ulysses has achieved
The sack of Ballio's sacred citadel.[18]

Ballio   Give me your lucky hand, you lucky fellow,   1065
Simo.

Simo   What's up?

Ballio   Now—

Simo   What now?

Ballio   No problem!

Simo   Why?
Did my man come here?

---

[18]In depicting Pseudolus as a warrior at Troy, Simo refers to Ulysses' legendary theft of the Palladium, Minerva's sacred image. I have simplified the allusion.

Pseudolus

| Ballio | No. |

Simo   Then what's so good?

Ballio   Your twenty mina coins are safe and sound—
         The bet you made today with Pseudolus.

Simo   I'd like to think so.

Ballio   I'll pay up myself,   1070
         If your slave gets possession of that girl
         Or else conveys her to your son, as pledged.
         Oh, Herc! Please bet me! I'm itching to give my word,
         To reassure you that your money's safe.
         You can even keep the woman as a gift.   1075

Simo   I see no risk in closing out the deal
         On those conditions. (*formally*) Twenty minas do you
         Swear to give?

Ballio   I do.

Simo   That's not so bad!
         But have you ever met Pseudolus?

Ballio   Sure, with your son.

Simo   What did he say to you? What words did he use?   1080

Ballio   Theater rubbish, standard pimp abuse
         From the comic stage, well known to every child:
         He called me a dirty double-crossing crook.

Simo   He didn't tell a lie.

Ballio   So I wasn't angry.
         How can it matter if you bad-mouth a man   1085
         Who doesn't care and doesn't contradict?

Simo   All right, I'd like to hear why he's no problem.

Ballio   Because he'll never nab the girl from me:

	He can't! Remember I told you she was sold,	
	Some time back, to a captain from Macedon?	1090

Simo   I do.

Ballio   Well, sir, his slave brought me the cash,
         With a sign in sealing wax—

Simo   Go on.

Ballio   —As prearranged by the officer and me.
         He took away the girl a while ago.

Simo   Is that the honest truth?

Ballio   The what? From me?   1095

Simo   Watch out it's not some fabricated scheme.

Ballio   The seal and the letter make me positive.
         He took her and left for Sicyon just now.

Simo   Great Herc! Great work! I can hardly wait to appoint
         Pseudolus Mayor of Millstone Colony.[19]   1100
         (*looking offstage, left*)
         But who's this in the cloak?

Ballio   I've no idea.
         Let's watch to see where he goes and what he does.

Act IV, Scene 7

The real HARPAX *enters* (*stage right*) *singing a self-congratulatory solo.* BALLIO
and SIMO *are not quite close enough to understand his words; at first,* BALLIO *will
take him to be a young client, ripe for the plucking.*

Harpax   I find corrupt those slaves who flout
         Or disregard their master's rules.

---

[19]As the first "colonist" sent to forced labor in the gristmill, Pseudolus will give his name to
the new settlement.

Some can't perform a task without
  A blunt reminder: stupid fools!
No sooner out of master's sight   1105
    They think they're free,
    At liberty
    To wench and brawl
    And squander all
They have; but they're still slaves, all right!
The only talent they possess
Is getting by on craftiness.   1110
I've had no contact with that mob:
I've kept my distance, done my job.
In master's absence, I assume
My master's standing in the room.
I'm frightened when he's nowhere near;
When he's around I feel no fear.

And now for this assignment here!   1115

I remained in the tavern for Syrus' call—
  He had taken the letter and told me to wait;
I expected some word when the pimp arrived home,
  But the man hasn't come and it's now getting late.
So I'm here to discover just what's going on;
  Did he take me, perhaps, for a bit of a ride?   1120
Now my sensible move is to knock on the door
  And to summon somebody who may be inside.

(*waving the purse, as he moves toward Ballio's door*)
  I want the pimp to take this fee
  And send the girl away with me.

Ballio   (*whispering to* SIMO) Hey there!

Simo   What is it?

Ballio   The man is mine.

Simo   How so?

Ballio   Because this catch looks fine.

He's got the dough, he wants a doll;
I'm going to crunch him, bones and all.   1125

Simo   Will you devour him on the spot?

Ballio   Yes, while he's fresh and piping hot.
For while he's in a giving mood,
Not to eat him would be rude.

Upstanding fellows make me poor,
And sinners make me fat;
The public likes the hero type,
But I prefer the rat.

Simo   (*aside*) The gods will give you living hell
For wickedness like that!   1130

Harpax   (*aside*) I'm wasting time; I'll give these doors a swat,
To see if Ballio's at home or not.

Ballio   (*to* SIMO) It's Venus who confers these joys,
Who sends me all these good-time boys,
These damn-the-cost, let's-go-for-brokers,
Self-indulgent, carefree jokers.
Lads who eat and drink and screw,
In temperament they're not like you:
A pleasure-hater so repressed
You spoil all pleasure for the rest.   1135

Harpax   (*shouting at the door*) Hey, anybody home?

Ballio   (*aside*) I think
He's heading straight toward my house.

[*Harpax*   (*knocking*) Hey, anybody home?

Ballio   Young man,
What debt are you collecting here?][20]
(*aside*) I'll get a load of loot from him;
I recognize my lucky charm.

---

[20]The bracketed lines are repetitive, and should perhaps be deleted from the text.

Harpax   (*knocking loudly*) Will no one open?

Ballio   You in the cloak!
What debt are you collecting here?

Harpax   I'm after Ballio the pimp,
The master of this residence.   1140

Ballio   Whoever you may be, young fellow,
Spare the effort of that search.

Harpax   Why so?

Ballio   Because he's here before you,
Face to face and large as life.

Harpax   (*pointing to* SIMO) You're him?

Simo   (*outraged*) Watch out, you dressed-up lout,
Beware my crooked walking stick
And point your filthy finger this way:
(*indicating* BALLIO) Here's the pimp.

Ballio   (*indicating* SIMO) And here's the gent.
But gentle sir, you've often heard
The howls of raging creditors,   1145
When you've been penniless except
For what this pimp's provided you.

Harpax   Why don't you talk to me?

Ballio   O.K.,
I'm talking. What do you want?

Harpax   For you to take some money.

Ballio   Give!
My hand is constantly outstretched.

Harpax   Here, then. Take these silver minas—
Five, all counted and correct.

My master, Polymachaeroplagides,   1150
Said I should bring them here to you,
The sum he owed, and you should send
Phoenicium away with me.

Ballio   Your master?

Harpax   That's correct.

Ballio   The soldier?

Harpax   Yes, that's right.

Ballio   From Macedon?

Harpax   Exactly so.

Ballio   Sent you to me?
Polymachaeroplagides?

Harpax   You speak the truth.

Ballio   Instructing you
To give me this cash?

Harpax   If you're in fact
Pimp Ballio.

Ballio   And told you then
To take the woman away from me?   1155

Harpax   Yes.

Ballio   Did he say Phoenicium?

Harpax   Your memory is excellent!

Ballio   Wait here!
I'll soon be back.

Harpax   Well, hurry up;

Be quick! I'm in a rush. You see
How late in the day it is.

Ballio   I do;
But still I want this man's advice.
Just wait right here, I'll soon
Be back to see you.
(*taking* SIMO *aside*) What now, Simo?
What'll we do? He's caught in the act,
This man who brought the moneybag.   1160

Simo   How so?

Ballio   Don't you understand?

Simo   My ignorance is absolute.

Ballio   Your Pseudolus has hired this man
To play the role of messenger
From Macedon.

Simo   Have you received
His moneybag?

Ballio   Is seeing believing?

Simo   Say! In dealing with those spoils,
Remember to give half to me:
Friends should share and share alike.

Ballio   Good grief! The whole amount is yours.   1165

Harpax   (*impatiently*) How soon will you attend to me?

Ballio   (*aloud*) Hang on!
(*sotto voce*) What do you suggest now, Simo?

Simo   Let's have a little fun and games
With this fictitious courier;
We'll keep it up until he comes
To realize the joke's on him.

Ballio	(*to* SIMO) Just follow me.
	(*to* HARPAX) Well, well! So you're
	His slave, you say?

Harpax   Most certainly.

Ballio   What was your purchase price?

Harpax   His valor
Won me on the battlefield.   1170
I was commanding officer
In the place where I was born, back home.

Simo   Did he ransack the city jail,
The place where you were born, back home?

Harpax   If you speak insulting words to me,
You'll get them back.

Ballio   How long a time
Did it take to come from Sicyon?

Harpax   I arrived the second day, at noon.

Ballio   Holy Herc! You made good time!

Simo   The man's as speedy as can be: 1175
When you look at his calves, you know he's fit—
To wear great thumping ankle-chains.

Ballio   Tell me, were you accustomed to sleep
In a cradle as a little boy?

Simo   Of course he was.

Ballio   And had you the habit
Of doing (tut, tut!) . . . you know what I mean?

Simo   Tut, tut! Of course he had.

Harpax   Are you both
Quite sane?

Ballio   A probing question now:
At night, when the captain took the watch
And you stood guard along with him,   1180
Did his sword-blade always fit
Inside your scabbard perfectly?

Harpax   Go hang yourself!

Ballio   You'll get your chance
At hanging soon enough today.

Harpax   Either bring me out the girl
Or else return the money.

Ballio   Wait!

Harpax   Why wait?

Ballio   Tell us about this cloak:
How much was the rental fee?

Harpax   The which?

Simo   What does it cost to hire a sword?

Harpax   (*aside*) These men need their heads examined![21]   1185

Ballio   Don't leave—

Harpax   Let go!

Ballio   That hat: what price
Will it fetch its owner for the day?

Harpax   What "owner"? Are you raving mad?
I own these clothes; I bought them as
My private things.

Ballio   You've got your only
Private things between your legs.

---

[21] Literally, "These men need a dose of hellebore."

Harpax   *(aside)* These gents are smeared with oil; they need
        A good old-fashioned rubbing down.   1190

Ballio   Answer this question, in the name
        Of Herc (I'm very serious!):
        What are your wages? At what pittance
        Were you hired by Pseudolus?

Harpax   Who is that Pseudolus?

Ballio   Your coach,
        Who trained you in this stratagem,
        So you could use more stratagems
        To snatch the girl away from me.

Harpax   What Pseudolus? What stratagems
        Do you keep going on about?   1195
        I haven't the faintest notion who
        He is.

Ballio   Come on, away with you!
        Today there'll be no profit here
        For swindlers. Just tell Pseudolus
        Another fellow snatched the spoils,
        The first Harpax who came along.

Harpax   Honest to Pol, I'm really Harpax.

Ballio   Honest to Pol, you want to be.
        This is a swindle, pure and simple.

Harpax   I've handed you the moneybag;   1200
        When I first came some time ago,
        I gave the token to your slave,
        Right here before your door—the letter
        Signed with the portrait of my master.

Ballio   You gave a letter to my slave?
        Which slave?

Harpax   Syrus was his name.

Ballio	(*to* SIMO) This swindle's based on more than nonsense:
	It's been thought out wickedly.
	That scoundrel of a Pseudolus!
	How cleverly he's planned it all!

Ballio   (*to* SIMO) This swindle's based on more than nonsense:
It's been thought out wickedly.
That scoundrel of a Pseudolus!   1205
How cleverly he's planned it all!
He gave him the exact amount
Of money that the captain owed,
And dressed the fellow up like this
So he could take away the girl.
(*aloud*) The real Harpax personally
Brought that letter to me here.

Harpax   My name is Harpax, and I am
The Macedonian captain's slave.   1210
I've not been guilty of a single
Wicked or deceitful deed,
And I've no knowledge or awareness
Of your precious Pseudolus.

Simo   Barring a miracle, old pimp,
You've forfeited the girl for good.

Ballio   Ye gods, I'm getting really scared,
The more I listen to his words.
Ye gods, that Syrus fellow, too,
Has left my heart frigidified—   1215
The one who took the token in.
It's a wonder if he's not Pseudolus.
(*to* HARPAX) Hey, you, what did he look like, then,
The man you gave the token to?

Harpax   Bright red hair, protruding belly,
Rather swarthy, chubby calves,
With large head, ruddy face, sharp eyes,
And utterly enormous feet.

Ballio   You killed me when you reached those feet!   1220
It was Pseudolus himself.
I'm done for! Now I'm dying, Simo.

Harpax   I won't let you die, by Herc,
Unless the money's paid me back—
All twenty minas.

Simo	In addition, Twenty minas more for me.
Ballio	(*to* SIMO) So will you take away the prize That I put forward as a joke?
Simo	From wicked men it's right to take All loot and lucre that they make.
Ballio	At least hand over Pseudolus.
Simo	Hand over Pseudolus to you? What harm's he done? Did I not tell you A hundred times to watch for him?
Ballio	He ruined me.
Simo	He sentenced me To pay a twenty-mina fine.
Ballio	What shall I do now?
Harpax	Give me The money, then go hang yourself.
Ballio	Damn you! Follow me this way, please, To the forum; I'll pay up.
Harpax	I follow.
Simo	What about me?
Ballio	All foreigners get paid Today; but citizens, tomorrow. Pseudolus convened a court That put me on trial for life or death,[22] When he dispatched that other man To steal the girl from me today. (*to* HARPAX) Follow me. (*to audience*) But don't you wait

1225

1230

---

[22]Plautus' Roman reference is to the Comitia Centuriata, the assembly that had jurisdiction on capital charges.

For me to take this road back home.
The way life's gone, I've now decided
Alley travel's best for me.   1235

Harpax If you only walked at the rate you talked,
We'd have reached the forum long ago. (*exit stage left*)

Ballio My happy birthday soon will be
My gloomy death-day. Woe is me! (*exit*)

Act IV, Scene 8

Simo I've hit him up just fine, the way
My slave has hit his enemy.
Now I intend to lie in wait
For Pseudolus—not the way it's done
In other plays, where people lurk   1240
With whips and prods; I'll go inside
To find the twenty minas that
I promised if he did the job.
I'll pay him of my own free will.
The creature is so very clever,
Very cunning, very sly.
Pseudolus has quite surpassed
The Trojan horse, Ulysses too.

I'll get the money all prepared;
Then Pseudolus will be ensnared.[23]   1245
(*exit into his own house*)

---

[23]If taken at its face value, this comment seems inconsistent with what Simo has just said. Does he still hope to outwit Pseudolus by means of some trick or snare? There is a similar mysterious allusion in line 1292.

ACT V

Enter PSEUDOLUS, *stage right, in wild disarray; he is wearing a garland and has obviously been drinking nonstop since he was last seen.*

Act V, Scene 1

Pseud.   What's up, feet? My word, feet![24]
You're acting absurd, feet.
Do you really suppose I'll be offered a hand
When I wobble because you're unable to stand?
    If I stumble and fall,
       My tumble is all
          Your fault!
Well, moving at last? Hey, foot, I feel
You need your backside kicked, you heel.
That's the trouble with wine: it always knows   1250
Like a sneaky wrestler, to tackle the toes.

So help me Pollux, I do declare
I've gone on a simply spectacular tear!

Such an elegant spread, good taste sublime,
A marvellous host and a marvellous time.
No need for a rambling rhetorical style: 1255
Parties like this make life worthwhile!
All forms of pleasure, all manner of love;
The next best thing to heaven above.

Two lovers locked in love's embrace,
    With lips engaged and tongues entwined;   1260

---

[24] I intend these two lines to be read jerkily, in imitation of Plautus' bacchiac tetrameter: "Whăt's úp, feét? Mў wórd, feét! / Yoŭ're áctíng ăbsúrd, feét."

Two partners snuggling breast to breast,
A couple with coupling on their mind.

A snow-white hand, a toast, a sip,
Sweet cup of love and fellowship.

No hateful or obnoxious guest,
   No idiotic bore;
Just perfumes, unguents, pretty ribbons,
   Floral wreaths galore,   1265
Provided in profusion there—
   Don't ask me any more.

   That's the way
   We spent the day,
Young master and I, getting happy and tight,
   After I
   Accomplished my
Objective by putting the foe to flight.   1270

There I left them wining and dining,
   Reclining and fondling their ladies of leisure;
My sweetheart was acting the life of the party,
   Indulging herself with the utmost of pleasure.

I rose to leave; "Come, dance!" they cried.
   I gave a sort of jiggle,
This way; with expert skill I tried
   The Asiatic wiggle.[25]   1275
All bundled in my frilly cloak,
I did these steps (a silly joke);
They clapped, they shouted out "Encore!"
"Come back, we want a little more!"
I had my doubts, but just the same
Continued with my foolish game:
Parading for my girl, like this,
So she would offer me a kiss,
I pirouetted—and I fell!
That was my frolic's sad farewell;

---

[25] Ionic dancing was proverbial for its immodesty and immorality.

For while I struggled, *oops!* Watch out!
I shit my cloak (or just about).
Sweet Pollux, how they roared at me
For such a loss of dignity!   1280

I'm given a jug: I take a quaff.
I change my cloak, get that one off;
I head for home, and home I'll stay
Till this hangover goes away.

So long, young boss! Old boss must learn
    The bargain's satisfied.
(*knocking on his own door*)
Hey, open up, somebody, hey!
    Tell Simo I'm outside.

Act V, Scene 2

Simo   (*cautiously opening his door*)
        Some wretch at the door is calling me.   1285
        What's this? How come? What do I see?

Pseud. Your Pseudolus, garlanded and stewed.

Simo   (*aside*) That's frank, at least. Some attitude!
        Is he scared on my account? No, sir!
        I wonder, should I growl or purr?   1290
        (*pointing to a purse that he is carrying*)
        This moneybag rules out brute force;
        I hope to save it still, of course.

Pseud. (*approaching* SIMO)
        Good man, meet bad man: how do you do.

Simo   God bless you, Pseudolus! (*recoiling*) Phew!
        Get lost!

Pseud.   Hey, why am I rejected?

Simo   What the hell had you expected,
        Drunk and belching in my face?   1295

Pseud.   Just hold me gently, please, in case
I crash. How can you fail to see
That I am smashed quite smashingly?

Simo   What gall is this, to come here tight,
A wreath on your head, in broad daylight?

Pseud.   It gives me pleasure. (*belches again*)

Simo   Pleasure, sure!
You're pleased to belch in my face once more.   1300

Pseud.   Belching's beautiful. Don't be a pain!

Simo   I think, you rascal, you've the power
To guzzle Massic wine and drain
Four harvests in a single hour.

Pseud.   "In winter," add.[26]

Simo   All right, not bad!   1305
From where exactly should I say
You steered your loaded barge this way?

Pseud.   From a bash with your son.
Oh, Simo, what fun
To cheat Ballio!
My mission's accomplished
According to plan.

Simo   You're a terrible man!   1310

Pseud.   The girl's doing this (*a lewd gesture*).
She's in bed with your boy
And she's actually free.

Simo   I know the whole story;
No need to tell me.

---

[26]Because the Romans divided the daylight period into twelve hours, regardless of season, winter hours were of shorter duration.

Pseud.   Then where is my money
            And why the delay?

Simo   You've got right on your side.
            I admit it; I'll pay.

            (SIMO *hands the purse to* PSEUDOLUS.)

Pseud.   You said I'd never get it, yet it's mine.
            (*pointing to his own shoulder*)
            Just load this fellow up and fall in line.   1315

Simo   (*to audience*) Load him up?

Pseud.   That's what I said.

Simo   (*to audience*) May I beat him up instead?
            Will he pinch my purse and laugh at me, the swine?

Pseud.   Woe to the vanquished![27]

Simo   All right, turn your shoulder.

            (*Humiliated,* SIMO *places the purse over* PSEUDOLUS' *shoulder, and
            falls to his knees to beg for mercy.*)

Pseud.   Ah!

Simo   I never thought I would become
            A suppliant at your feet. Oh dear! Oh dear!

Pseud.   Oh, stop it!

Simo   I hurt!

Pseud.   If you didn't hurt, I would.   1320

Simo   Will you take this purse from master, Pseudolus, friend?

---

[27] *Vae victis,* the proverbial saying of the Gallic chieftain Brennus after the capture of Rome in
387 B.C.

Pseud.   With all the feeling in my heart and soul!

Simo   Please give me a tiny refund; you agree?

Pseud.   A greedy fellow: you can call me that,
For you won't get a penny richer from this purse.
You'd feel no pity for my wretched back,
If I had not achieved my goal today.

Simo   Someday, sure as I live, I'll get even with you!

Pseud.   Why do you threaten me? My skin is tough.   1325

Simo   Then go ahead. (*starting to leave*)

Pseud.   All right, come back.

Simo   What for?

Pseud.   Come back, that's all; no trick involved.

Simo   I'm here.

Pseud.   Come, join me for a drink together.

Simo   Me?

Pseud.   Just do as I tell you. If you come, I'll give you
Half or even more of your money back.

Simo   I'll come; conduct me where you will.

Pseud.   Well, then. This business hasn't made you cross   1330
At me or my young master, has it, boss?

Simo   Of course not!

Pseud.   Step this way; I'll follow you.

Simo   Perhaps you should invite the audience, too.

Pseud. Those cheapskates never have invited me;
Why offer them our hospitality?
(*to audience*)
    But if you say
    You liked our play,
And cheer our company before you go,
Then I'll invite you—to tomorrow's show.   1335
                    (*exeunt omnes*)

RUDENS (THE ROPE)

Introduction to *Rudens*

Rudens (*The Rope*) is regarded by many as Plautus' finest play. It is certainly one of his most unusual and interesting. With its setting on the wild North African coast, its romantic atmosphere of storm and shipwreck, its lonely temple and farmer's cottage, and its unique chorus of rustic fishermen, it is a far cry from the typical urban comedies of the Roman stage. The play is particularly impressive for its imaginative integration of stage setting with dramatic action and character development. In this respect, it has often been compared to Shakespeare's *The Tempest,* a play that may have drawn more than a little of its inspiration from *Rudens.*

Plautus' Latin title is derived from the trailing fisherman's rope employed as a brilliant stage property in Act IV, Scene 3, where two slaves engage in a prolonged verbal tussle and physical tug-of-war for the possession of a newly discovered treasure trove. The title of Diphilus' Greek original is unknown, but it may have alluded in some way to the wickerwork satchel or trunk in which the lost treasures were stored. Although *Rudens* cannot be securely dated within Plautus' career, the extent and quality of the lyric passages suggest that he was at the peak of his craft.

As the Prologue figure, Arcturus, tells us explicitly, this comedy is a moral tale, depicting the triumph of virtue over wickedness in a world ruled by a benevolent Providence (Jupiter and his multitude of cosmic agents). Daemones, a decent and honorable old man, has had his daughter kidnapped in infancy, has suffered bankruptcy and exile from his native Athens, and is now languishing on a remote farm outside Cyrene. As a result of a devastating heaven-sent storm, he becomes reunited with his long-lost daughter, thereby saving her from the clutches of the villainous pimp who has enslaved her. The daughter, Palaestra, and her companion slave Ampelisca discover that their terrifying immersion in the sea has been, surprisingly, a genuine purification; for it is a necessary prelude to their transformation from unwilling sexual merchandise into free young women, a change effected under the sympathetic influence of the goddess Venus. The pimp Labrax is suitably penalized for his duplicity and greed, though Daemones' humanity is such that even the villain of the piece is not harshly punished; indeed, Labrax is invited to share the old gentleman's dinner table at the close of the play.

Although the play is first and foremost a comic entertainment, with many vastly amusing scenes, it has a serious aspect that is not often to be found in Plautine drama. The pure young Palaestra is scarcely a comic character at all, as the poet makes clear in the poignant and pathetic monody that marks her first appearance. She has even been described as a symbolic figure, whose rescue and recognition are a re-enactment of Venus' archetypal birth from the sea.[1] Whether the guiding hand is mainly that of Diphilus or of Plautus, the play puts far more emphasis on Palaestra's loving relationship with her companion Ampelisca than on any romantic feelings that she may have for her young Athenian suitor, Plesidippus. Her urgent priorities are to escape the sexual bondage of Labrax and to discover the parents from whom she has long been separated. If modern readers are disappointed that there are no scenes of interaction between the two young lovers, they should realize that the dramatic focus is entirely on the climactic recognition, not on any subsequent marriage. Lacking Palaestra's powerful motivation, Ampelisca is a more earthy and amusing character, but she too is portrayed as a thoroughly admirable young woman. At the end of the play, we heartily applaud Daemones' decision to buy her freedom, presumably so that she may marry Plesidippus' former slave Trachalio.

The humor of the play is sustained in large measure by three excellent slave roles, the urban (and urbane) Trachalio and his rustic counterparts, the surly Sceparnio and the doggedly persistent Gripus. The pimp Labrax and his Sicilian guest Charmides are as richly comic as any characters on the Plautine stage.

The action of the play has two distinct movements. Acts I to III depict the two young women's escape from the sea and their rescue, at the temple of Venus, from the pimp's control. Acts IV and V portray the discovery of Labrax's trunk and its role in Palaestra's reunion with her father. There is some disjunction between these two segments of the plot, apparent in the separation of the slave roles Sceparnio and Gripus. No one, however, is likely to fault *Rudens* for lack of unity. Quite apart from its coherent story line, the play is magnificently united by the ever-present sea, as dominant in poetic imagery as it is in dramatic action.

This comedy provides unusual opportunities and challenges for the mod-

[1] Eleanor Winsor Leach, "Plautus' *Rudens:* Venus Born from a Shell," *Texas Studies in Literature and Language* 15 (1974): 915–931.

ern stage director and set designer. Very likely Plautus' stage was a simple bare platform that left the rocky coastline entirely to the audience's imagination. (Incidentally, the audience out front is sitting squarely in the middle of the raging sea.) A modern producer might make effective use of ramps and rocky mounds in order to enhance and enliven those scenes that take place somewhere between the water's edge and the higher ground (I.3–4, II.6, IV.3).

With misgivings, I have followed the general consensus of modern scholars in placing the entrance to and from Cyrene (both town and harbor) on stage right, and the route to and from the shore on stage left; possibly these directions should be reversed, since line 156 makes better sense if the shore route lies to stage right.

The standard scholarly edition of the play is Friedrich Marx, *Plautus Rudens: Text und Kommentar* (Berlin, 1928; repr. Amsterdam: Hakkert, 1959). There has not been a major commentary in English since that of Edward A. Sonnenschein (Oxford: Clarendon Press, 1891), abridged and reissued as a school edition in 1901. Considerable advice on stage production and useful notes can be found in H. C. Fay's edition, *T. Macci Plauti Rudens* (London: University Tutorial Press, 1969; repr. Bristol: Bristol Classical Press, 1983).

CHARACTERS

ARCTURUS	a brilliant star; speaker of the Prologue
DAEMONES	a virtuous old Athenian, now exiled in Cyrene
SCEPARNIO	a slave of Daemones'
PLESIDIPPUS	a young Athenian, in love with Palaestra
TRACHALIO	a slave of Plesidippus'
PALAESTRA	a pathetic young woman; Daemones' daughter and now Labrax's slave
AMPELISCA	Palaestra's companion in misery
PTOLEMOCRATIA	a priestess of Venus
LABRAX	an unscrupulous pimp and slave dealer
CHARMIDES	an old Sicilian, Labrax's guest
FISHERMEN	anonymous residents of Cyrene
GRIPUS	a fisherman slave of Daemones'
TURBALIO	a flogging-slave of Daemones'
SPARAX	another flogging-slave of Daemones'
FRIENDS OF PLESIDIPPUS	silent roles

PROLOGUE

The stage depicts a remote seashore near Cyrene, on the North African coast. On a rugged hillside above the sea stand two isolated buildings, a temple of Venus (stage right) and a humble farmhouse owned by Daemones (stage left). An altar of Venus stands within the temple precinct. There is no other sign of human habitation.

The play opens with the appearance, perhaps on the temple roof, of ARCTURUS, *brightest star in the constellation Boötes. As befits a heavenly being of his magnitude, he wears a resplendent and dazzling costume.*

Arctur.	The almighty Overlord of land and sea
	I serve, a citizen of the celestial sphere.
	Behold a brilliant stellar personage,
	A star that always mounts the stage on cue,

Here, as in heaven. Arcturus is my name.   5
By night I gleam in heaven among the gods;
In mortal company I stroll by day.
Other stars come down to earth as well;
Jupiter, commander-in-chief of gods and men,
Assigns us vantage points around the world   10
To view your conduct and your character,
So that he may confer prosperity.
If men engage false witnesses to bring
False suit, or dare deny a debt in court,
We scribble their names and send them up to Jove.   15
Each day he knows the troublemakers here.
When scoundrels press demands by perjury
Or gain corrupt awards before a judge,
These judgments Jove adjudicates again:
His fines exceed by far the fruits of fraud.   20
(Good folk get written down in other lists.)
Wicked people try to persuade themselves
That Jove can be swayed by gifts and sacrifice.
They're wasting effort and expense; he won't
Accept peace offerings from perjurers.   25

An honest person will receive forgiveness
Far ahead of any begging crook.
So here's my advice to all you virtuous types
Who pass your lives in piety and trust:
Keep up the good work: you'll be glad you did!   30

Now for the plot—the reason I've come here.
Our Greek play's author, Diphilus, named this town
Cyrene. Over there lives Daemones,
In a cottage on a farm beside the sea.
Though banished from Athens, he's not a bad old sort.   35
Wrongdoing didn't cost him his fatherland;
He got entangled helping others out,
And wrecked his well-earned wealth with decency.
He'd lost his daughter, a darling little girl,
Sold off by pirates to a dreadful man,   40
A pimp, who brought her to Cyrene here.
A young Athenian (her compatriot)
Once glimpsed her going home from music school,
And fell in love. He called upon her pimp,
Secured the girl at a thirty-mina price,   45
Made partial payment and received a pledge.

True to form, the pimp gave not a fig for faith,
And scorned his solemn promise to the lad.
He's got a guest, a soul mate from Sicily,
A mean old crook who'd sell his own hometown.   50
This guest begins to praise that gorgeous girl
And the other luscious ladies in the house.
He starts coaxing the pimp to accompany him
To Sicily. Men live for pleasure there,
He says; a person there can soon get rich;   55
There courtesans command the highest price.
He makes his case. On the sly, a ship is hired,
The pimp piles all his earthly goods aboard
By night; to the lad who'd bought the girl from him
He says he wants to pay a vow to Venus   60
(This is her temple here) and asks the boy
To come to lunch. But he himself on the instant
Boards the ship, packs off his merchandise.
Other people tell the lad the news:

The pimp has flown. Our hero runs to the dock;   65
Those rascals' ship is now far out to sea.

When I, yours truly, saw the girl dragged off,
Deliverance I brought her; for the pimp, dismay.
I roared a wintry blast and roiled the waves.
For I'm Arcturus, a ferocious star: 70
Fierce when I rise; while setting, fiercer far.

Now both men, pimp and guest, hang on for dear life,
Stranded on a rock: their ship's destroyed.
But our heroine and her companion slave
Leapt, terrified, into a little boat.   75
Now the waves are washing them ashore
Toward this man's house—the exiled gentleman,
Whose roof and tiles got torn off by the wind.
That's his slave coming out the door.
The lad's arriving soon; you'll see him here,   80
The one who struck the bargain for the girl.

Take care; may your adversaries lose their nerve!

                                        (*exit*)

ACT I

The slave SCEPARNIO, *who has already appeared at the door of Daemones' cottage, now comes outside to fulfill his master's orders. He is carrying a shovel and talking to himself.*

Act I, Scene 1

Scepar.   Ye gods eternal, what an awful storm
              Lord Neptune visited on us last night!
              The wind unroofed the house. Did I say wind?   85
              A real production by Euripides![2]
              It wrenched the tiles right off the roof,
              Providing windows to enhance our light.

Act I, Scene 2

SCEPARNIO *gets ready for his task of digging clay so as to make new tiles. Enter* PLESIDIPPUS, *the young Athenian lover, from the harbor of Cyrene (stage right). He is accompanied by three silent* FRIENDS, *dressed in military cloaks and carrying swords.*

Plesid.   Although I've dragged you from your proper jobs,
             This project failed in its desired result: 90
             I didn't catch the pimp down by the docks.
             But I've not sluggishly abandoned hope;
             That's why, my friends, I've kept you on a while.
             I've come here now to check out Venus' shrine,
             Where he declared he'd offer sacrifice.   95

Scepar.   (*oblivious of* PLESIDIPPUS *and his three friends*)
             If I'm smart I'll fashion this confounded clay.

---

[2]Literally, "It was the *Alcumena* by Euripides." That lost tragedy apparently featured a notorious storm.

224

Plesid.	Somebody's talking.

(*Enter the old man* DAEMONES, *who comes out of his house to supervise his slave.*)

Daemo.	Hey, Sceparnio!
Scepar.	Who's calling my name?
Daemo.	The one who paid cash for you.
Scepar.	(*aside*) You'd think I was your servant, Daemones.
Daemo.	We must have loads of clay, dig loads of soil. 100

It's wholly apparent my house must be re-roofed;
It's wholly transparent—holey as a sieve.

Plesid.	(*moving closer to make his presence known*)

Father, good day—to both of you.

Daemo.	Good day.
Scepar.	Are you male or female sex, who call him "father"?
Plesid.	I'm a man.
Scepar.	Find "father" somewhere else. 105
Daemo.	I had one daughter once, but I lost her;

I never had a son.

Plesid.	The gods will give—
Scepar.	—you holy hell, by Herc, whoever you are,

Who babble on and bother busy folk!

Plesid.	(*pointing to the farmhouse*)

Do you live over here?

Scepar.	What's that to you? 110

You casing us to burglarize the place?

Plesid.	A slave must be free of fault and far from poor
	To chatter when his master is around
	Or speak so rudely to a gentleman.

Scepar.	A gentleman must be brash and brazen-faced	115
	To barge in uninvited at a house	
	That owes him nothing.	

Daemo.   Quiet, Sceparnio!
What do you want, young man?

Plesid.   A thrashing for him,
For butting in like that when his master's here.
If it's not a nuisance, I'd like to ask you   120
A question or two.

Daemo.   I'll try to help, but I'm busy.

Scepar. (*menacing* PLESIDIPPUS)
Why not go to the swamp and cut some reeds
To thatch the house, while the weather's fine?

Daemo.   Shut up!
(*to* PLESIDIPPUS) Just let me know what you need.

Plesid.   Please tell me, then,
Have you seen a gray and frizzy-headed type,   125
A lousy, lying toady?

Daemo. (*surveying the audience*) Many of those!
That sort has made my life a misery.

Plesid. The fellow I mean brought two young ladies here
With him to Venus' temple, and was planning
Holy rites, today or yesterday.   130

Daemo. No, my lad, for several days I've seen
Nobody sacrificing there. They can't
Do that without my knowledge: always they want
Water, firewood, saucepans, knives, or spits,
Or boiling pots, or something. Why waste words?   135
I dug this well for Venus, not for me.

Plesid.   (*tragically*) Your dreadful discourse has declared my doom.

Daemo.   By Hercules, I only wish you well.

Scepar.   Hey, you! You scrounging temple-hanger-on,   140
            You'd better order lunch prepared at home.

Daemo.   Were you invited here to dine, perhaps,
           And your luncheon host did not arrive?

Plesid.   That's right.

Scepar.   No damage, then, in going home unfed.
            Chase after Ceres and give Venus up: 145
            She handles love, but Ceres handles grain.

Plesid.   That fellow's made outrageous fun of me.

Daemo.   (*suddenly noticing activity on the coastline below*)
           Immortal gods! Who are those people there,
           Sceparnio, along the shore?

Scepar.   I'd say
            They've been invited to a farewell lunch.   150

Daemo.   Why so?

Scepar.   They took a bath last night to get ready.

Daemo.   Their ship's been torn apart at sea.

Scepar.   That's true;
            Just like our house and roof on land.

Daemo.   Dear me,
           Poor creatures! How those castaways can swim!   155

Plesid.   Where are these people, please?

Daemo.   This way, to the right.
           Do you see? Along the shore.

Plesid.   I see. (*to his* FRIENDS) Follow me!
I hope it's that damned fellow I'm looking for.
Take care.   (*They rush out, stage left.*)

Scepar. We can remember that without your help.
    (*looking out to sea in another direction*)
    Holy Palaemon, Neptune's acolyte,   160
    Esteemed confederate of Hercules!
    What dreadful sight is this?

Daemo.   What sight?

Scepar.   Young ladies,
    Two of them, sitting alone in a tiny boat.
    They're taking an awful pounding! Wow! Well done![3]
    The surge has steered their boat from reef to shore. 165
    A pilot couldn't have managed half as well.
    I don't remember seeing larger waves.
    They're safe if they avoid that foamy surge.
    Now's the danger, now! One's overboard!
    It's shallow; she'll easily wade out. Hurray!   170
    Do you see her, how the wave has tossed her out?
    She's on her feet and headed this way. She's safe.
    But now the other has tried to jump ashore.
    She's terrified; she's fallen to her knees!
    She's safely out of the water, high and dry.   175
    But she's turning to the right—the road to hell!
    She'll wander the day away.

Daemo.   What's that to you?

Scepar. If she falls off the cliff she's headed for,
    She can forgo all further wandering.   180

Daemo. If you plan to dine at their expense tonight,
    Look after them, I'd say, Sceparnio.
    If you're going to eat at my house, work for me.

---

[3]Marx (cited in the Introduction) assigned this line to Daemones, changing the following passage from a monologue by Sceparnio to a rapid exchange of dialogue between slave and master. Although this emendation is dramatically effective, it has no manuscript support.

Scepar.   That's fair enough.

Daemo.   Then step this way.

Scepar.   I come.
                    (*They enter Daemones' house.*)

Act I, Scene 3

Having scrambled up from the shore below, the dripping and disheveled PALAESTRA
*enters, stage left. Although she is officially a courtesan in the service of the pimp
Labrax, she is a pure, innocent, and vulnerable young woman. During her opening
soliloquy, she is unaware of the temple and farmhouse that are behind her, upstage.*

Palaes.   Contrived accounts of human pain
                    Can hardly make us feel   185
                That we're experiencing life,
                    Where agonies are real.
                If I'm a frightened castaway
                    In this uncertain land,
                Can my forlorn predicament
                    Be what the gods have planned?

                Is this the goal of my unhappy life?
                Is this requital for my piety?   190
                To bear such toil might well be toil enough
                If I'd abused my parents or the gods;
                But when I've diligently taken pains
                To do no wrong, the gods' repayment is
                Excessive, unbecoming, and unfair.
                Henceforth, what guidance will the wicked have   195
                If heaven so mistreats the innocent?

                I would be less unhappy if I knew
                That I or my parents had been criminals.
                But I'm tormented for my master's crime:
                It's his impiety that injures me.
                He lost his ship and everything he owned;
                These rags are the remnants of his property.   200
                And even she who shared my tiny boat

Has disappeared from sight. I'm quite alone.
If only she were safe and with me now,
At least her presence would relieve my pain.

What hope have I, what help, what strategy,
Alone in such a lonely wilderness? 205
Here are the reefs, and here the crashing sea,
But nowhere human company for me.

These clothes I wear are all my worldly wealth;
No food is here, no shelter's to be seen.
What hope can motivate me to survive?
This place is unfamiliar and unknown. 210
If someone from this region could at least
Reveal a road or footpath! I am so
Devoid of counsel, doubtful where to turn.
I see no cultivated field nearby.

I'm in the grip of bitter cold,
Uncertainty, and fright; 215
Dear parents, you are unaware
That I am in this plight.
A freeborn citizen was I,
A fact of little worth:
Could I be more enslaved right now
Had I been slave by birth?

My freedom's never done a scrap of good
To those who reared and loved me as a child!

Act I, Scene 4

As PALAESTRA *collapses in exhaustion and despair, enter* AMPELISCA *from the shore, stage left. Like her companion, she is very young and totally discouraged. Because of their physical condition and the nature of the rocky terrain, the two young women are not easily reunited.*

Ampel.   What deed could better serve my cause
Than snuffing out this dismal life? 220
My lot is wretched, and my breast

Is numbed with paralyzing cares.
In truth, I'm weary of my life,
All hope of consolation gone.

I've run a circuit round the seashore,
Crawling into every cranny,
Searching out my fellow slave
And tracking her with eyes, ears, voice.
Failing to find a trace of her,
I've no idea where to look;   225
So far I haven't met a soul
Whose answers might enlighten me.
No desert tracts on earth are more
Forlorn and desolate than these.
As long as I live, I'll never cease
My quest to find her in this life.

Palaes.   Whose voice is this
That sounds nearby?

Ampel.   I'm frightened! Who
Is speaking here?   230

Palaes.   Good Hope, assist me
Now, I pray.

Ampel.   Release me from
My dismal fears.

Palaes.   Surely a woman's voice has reached my ears.

Ampel.   That is a woman! That's a woman's voice.

Palaes.   Not Ampelisca?

Ampel.   Palaestra, is that you?   235

Palaes.   Why don't I call her name, so she may hear?
Ampelisca!

Ampel.   Oh! Who is it?

Palaes.   Me: Palaestra.

Ampel.   Where are you?

Palaes.   I am now in dire distress.

Ampel.   Partner, my share of pain must equal yours.
I yearn to see you.

Palaes.   There you rival me.   240

Ampel.   Let's follow our voices, step by step. Where are you?

Palaes.   Here I am. Come this way, straight ahead.

Ampel.   With all my heart.

Palaes.   Give me your hand.

Ampel.   Here, take it.

Palaes.   Tell me, are you actually alive?

Ampel.   You make me want to go on living now,
When we're allowed to touch. It's hard to credit   245
That I'm holding you! Embrace me, please,
My hope! How light my burdens have become!

Palaes.   You took the very words out of my mouth.
We ought to leave here now.

Ampel.   Where shall we go?

Palaes.   Let's keep to the coastline.

Ampel.   Where you lead, I'll follow.   250
Must we traipse about in dripping clothes?

Palaes.   The here and now must be endured.
But what is this, I wonder?

Ampel.   What?

Palaes.   Please, look!
        Do you see this temple?

Ampel.   Where is it?

Palaes.   To the right.

Ampel.   I see a place appropriate for gods.   255

Palaes.   People can't be far away
        From here, it's such a lovely spot.
        I pray the unknown god may deign
        To rescue us from this ordeal,
        Thereby assisting women wretched,
        Needy, and oppressed by toil.

Act I, Scene 5

In the temple doorway appears the mature and imposing figure of PTOLEMO-
CRATIA, *Priestess of Venus.*

Ptolem.   Who can be praying for my Lady's help?
        The voice of suppliants brings me to the door.   260
        A good, obliging goddess they address,
        A Lady ever generous and kind.

Palaes.   We give you greeting, mother.

Ptolem.   And to you,
        Good day. But where can you have come from, girls?
        You're so bedraggled and so woebegone.   265

Palaes.   Just now, from over there, not far away;
        But we were brought here from some distance off.

Ptolem.   "On wooden steed o'er azure paths ye hied,"[4]
        No doubt.

---

[4] "On wooden steed" is a flowery circumlocution for "by ship." Is the priestess quoting some lost tragedy? She is probably not being facetious, since her diction is otherwise almost archaic in its dignity.

233

Palaes.   Exactly.

Ptolem.   Then you should have come
Arrayed in white, with ritual animals.   270
People don't approach our shrine this way!

Palaes. And where should we have found those animals,
When we have both been cast up from the sea?
In desperation we embrace your knees,
With unknown prospects in an unknown land.   275
Accept and shelter us beneath your roof;
Take pity on two pitiable girls,
Who have no place to go, no cause for hope,
Nothing in the world save what you see.

Ptolem. Give me your hands and stand up, both of you.   280
No woman's more compassionate than I.
But girls, my situation here is poor:
I find it hard to meet my personal needs,
And I serve Venus at my own expense.

Ampel. Is this a temple of Venus?

Ptolem.   That it is.
I'm spoken of as Priestess of the Shrine.   285
All my resources will be cordially
Shared with you, so far as means permit.

Palaes. Good mother, you show kind and generous
Consideration for us.

Ptolem.   As I should.
(*The three* WOMEN *go inside the temple.*)

ACT II

Several shabbily-dressed FISHERMEN *enter from the direction of Cyrene, stage right. Carrying rods, nets, and shellfish equipment, they perform an energetic choral dance.*

Act II, Scene 1

Fisher.   A poor man's life in all respects
        Is nasty and appalling,   290
     Particularly if he lacks
        A proper trade or calling.
     He must survive on what he owns:
        Necessity is galling!

     This get-up likely tells you our
        Financial situation;
     These hooks and fishing rods provide
        Our gainful occupation.
     We come here daily from the town
        To forage from the ocean;   295
     The sea's our wrestling ground, our gym,
        Our muscular devotion.

     We harvest oysters, limpets, whelks,
        And periwinkles tiny;
     Mussels, scallops, jellyfish,
        Sea urchins sharp and spiny.

     In rocky nooks we bait our hooks,
        A fishy foe pursuing;
     The sea provides our nourishment—
        Unless there's nothing doing.   300
     For if we don't catch any fish,

Then *we* get cleaned and salted;
Back home we head to sneak to bed,
And dinner's been defaulted.

Because the sea's now rough and wild,
Our case is hopeless, nearly;
Unless we catch some cockles soon,
Our dinner's over, clearly.
Let's venerate good Venus now:
May she regard us dearly.   305

Act II, Scene 2

Enter TRACHALIO, *Plesidippus' shrewd and resourceful slave, from the town (stage right).*

Trach.   *(to himself)* I've paid attention so as not
To miss my boss along the way;
He spoke of going to the harbor,
Telling me to come along
To meet him here at Venus' shrine.
But how convenient! Look! Some men
For me to question. I'll approach.

(aloud) Good day, ye pilferers of the deep,
Ye sons of cockle and of fishhook,   310
Famished tribe of humankind.
How are you doing? How are you dying?

Fisher.   The standard way for fishermen:
Of hunger, thirst, and cheating hope.

Trach.   Tell me, while you've been standing here,
Have you seen a young man arrive?
A lad of vigorous appearance,
Flushed complexion, powerful,
Who likely had three men in tow,
With military cloaks and swords?   315

Fisher.   Nobody matching your description
Has arrived, that we know of.

236

Trach.	Try this:

An old man, balding like Silenus,[5]
Sturdy build, protruding paunch,
With crooked eyebrows, forehead furrowed
In a frown—a nasty swindler,
Hated alike by gods and men,
Crammed full of criminal deceit,
Who'd be escorting two young ladies,
Quite attractive little things?   320

Fisher. If any person is endowed
With features such as you describe, ·
I think he'd better go get hanged
Instead of wasting Venus' time.

Trach. But if you've seen him, tell me.

Fisher. Really, no one's come this way.
Goodbye.   (*The* FISHERMEN *leave, stage left.*)

Trach.   Goodbye. (*to himself*) I thought so!
The crooked pimp has tricked my master,
Taken off to skip the country,   325
Boarded ship and snatched away
The women. I felt it in my bones!
He invited my young master here
To lunch, that sower of villainy!
Well, what could I do better now
Than wait here till the boss arrives?
Meanwhile, if I see this priestess
I'll just cross-examine her.
If she has any further knowledge
She can bring me up to date.   330

Act II, Scene 3

AMPELISCA *appears at the door of Venus' temple, carrying a pitcher; before encountering her old friend* TRACHALIO, *she speaks over her shoulder to the priestess inside the temple.*

---

[5]Silenus is the obese and drunken companion of Bacchus, often represented in literature and art.

Ampel.   I understand: you wanted me
         To knock on the door of this house beside
         The Temple of Venus, and to ask
         For water.

Trach.   (*waxing poetic*) Hark, what winged words
         Are wafted to my ears?

Ampel.   Oh, my!
         Who's speaking here?

Trach.   Whom do I see?
         Can this be Ampelisca coming
         Out of the temple?

Ampel.   Can this be
         Trachalio that I have glimpsed,
         Plesidippus' right-hand man?   335

Trach.   It's she!

Ampel.   It's he! Trachalio, hi!

Trach.   Hi, Ampelisca. How is life,
         Old girl?

Ampel.   The girl is young; life's bad.

Trach.   Be careful: mustn't talk that way!

Ampel.   All friends of wisdom should pursue
         The goal of uttering the truth.
         But where's your master, Plesidippus?
         Tell me, please.

Trach.   Hey, knock it off!
         As if he weren't inside!

Ampel.   I swear,
         He's not; he hasn't come at all.   340

Trach.   He hasn't come?

Ampel.	You're telling the truth.
Trach.	That isn't like me, Ampelisca. How soon now will lunch be ready?
Ampel.	Just what lunch do you have in mind?
Trach.	Presumably you're sacrificing Here.
Ampel.	What kind of dream is this?
Trach.	Well, Labrax certainly invited Plesidippus here for lunch, Your master and my boss.
Ampel.	Dear Pollux! Your account is not surprising: If he cheated gods and men, He simply acted like a pimp.
Trach.	You and my boss are not performing Sacrifices here?
Ampel.	Bull's-eye!
Trach.	Then what are you up to?
Ampel.	At a time When we were helpless and bereft, This priestess from the shrine of Venus Rescued us from mortal peril, Dire disaster, dread despair, And took us in, Palaestra and me.
Trach.	I must know, is Palaestra here, My master's ladylove?
Ampel.	That's right.
Trach.	Your message, Ampelisca dear, Is brimming with abundant charm.

345

350

> But I would really like to know
> About that danger you were in.

Ampel.   Our ship, my dear Trachalio,
        Got bashed and battered in the night.

Trach.   What ship? What story are you telling?

Ampel.   Haven't you heard? About the pimp?   355
        How he intended secretly
        To carry us away from here
        To Sicily, and how he loaded
        All his goods aboard a ship?
        Everything has perished now.

Trach.   How do you do, delightful Neptune!
        No one's cleverer than you
        At playing dice. You've obviously
        Made a most delicious throw:
        You've polished off a perjurer.   360
        But whereabouts is Labrax now?

Ampel.   I do believe he died from drinking:
        Last night, Neptune challenged him
        To fill his cup to overflowing.

Trach.   Holy Herc! I bet the fellow
        Had to chugalug his drink!
        Dear Ampelisca, love, how sweet
        You are, what honeyed words you speak!
        But how can it be that you and Palaestra
        Have survived?

Ampel.   I'll fill you in.   365
        In terror, she and I jumped down
        Into a skiff, because we saw
        Our ship was headed for the rocks.
        I hastily untied the rope
        While the men were panicking; the storm
        Took us and the skiff away from them,
        And off to the right. So we two girls

	Were tossed around by wind and wave,	
	Enduring an everlasting night	
	In misery of every kind.	370
	On point of death, blown in by winds,	
	Today we barely reached the shore.	

Trach. That's just like Neptune: an inspector
With discriminating taste.
If merchandise is second-rate,
He'll toss the whole lot overboard.

Ampel. I hope you shrivel up and die!

Trach. The same to you, dear Ampelisca. 375
I knew the pimp would act the way
He has; I often said as much.
I think I'll let my hair grow long
And go into business as a prophet.

Ampel. If you knew, did you take precautions,
You and your boss, to stop him going?

Trach. What could he do?

Ampel. Her lover, you ask me,
What could he do? He should have watched her
Day and night, been constantly
Upon his guard. So help me Castor, 380
Plesidippus' fine surveillance
Shows how much he really cared.

Trach. Why that remark?

Ampel. It's obvious.

Trach. But listen here! If someone goes
To a public bathhouse, never mind
How carefully he guards his clothes,
They still get stolen, just because
He doesn't know which way to look.
The thief can easily mark his prey;

| | The victim can't make out the thief. | 385 |
| | But take me to her. | |

Ampel.   Very well,
Just go inside the temple here,
You'll find her sitting, crying her eyes out.

Trach. That I'll find quite hard to take!
But why's she crying?

Ampel.   I'll explain.
She's in a state of agony
Because the pimp deprived her of
The tiny box where she kept clues
Enabling her to recognize
Her parents. Now she is afraid   390
It's gone forever.

Trach.   Where was that tiny
Little box?

Ampel.   Aboard the ship.
His lordship locked it in a trunk,
So she would never have a chance
To find out who her parents were.

Trach. What a barefaced, dirty trick
To force a girl to be a slave
Who should quite properly be free!

Ampel. Now it's undoubtedly gone down
With the ship to the bottom of the sea.   395
The pimp's reserves of silver and gold
Were all inside the trunk, as well.

Trach. Some fellow, I suspect, has dived in
To recover it.

Ampel.   That's why she's glum:
Those things of hers are gone forever.

Trach.	All the more reason, then, for me
	To go inside and cheer her up;
	I'll calm that state of agony.
	"When hope seems hopeless, many men
	Discover happiness again." 400
Ampel.	Still, "Hope will oftentimes deceive
	The many who in hope believe."
Trach.	So, "If on trouble we must feed,
	A pinch of patience we will need."
	I'm going in, unless you want—
Ampel.	Go on, get going.

(TRACHALIO *enters the temple.*)

                 I intend
To do as the priestess ordered me,
And ask for water here next door.
If I apply on her behalf,
She said, they'll give it right away.   405

Among old ladies I have known,
I've never seen one more deserving,
More entitled to good treatment
At the hands of gods and men.
How kind she was, how courteous;
How gladly and ungrudgingly
She took us in when we were frightened,
Soaking wet, in dire need,
Cast ashore on the brink of death!
You'd think we were her own two girls!   410
She pitched right in, tucked up her dress,
And heated water for our bath.

No more delay; I'll get the water
Here, as she instructed me.
Hello! Anyone at home? Will someone
Open the door and come outside?

Act II, Scene 4

SCEPARNIO *opens the door a crack to peer out suspiciously.*

Scepar.   Who's this fellow who's inflicting
        Wanton damage on our door?

Ampel.   I am.

Scepar.   Ha! What have we here?
        Hurrah! A lovely-looking girl.   415

Ampel.   Good day, young man.

Scepar.   A good good-day
        To you, young woman. (Young, indeed!)

Ampel.   I come to you—

Scepar.   I'll comfort *you,*
        If you come back again tonight—
        Most tenderly; I simply can't
        Give service at this time of day.
        What do you say, my merry maid?

Ampel.   Oh, stop! You're being too familiar
        With your hands.

Scepar.   Immortal gods!
        She's Venus' image, this one is!   420
        What laughter in her loving eyes!
        Well, well! An admirable complexion:
        Kind of a sharkish dinner—sorry,
        I meant kind of a darkish shimmer.[6]
        Admirable little breasts;
        A mouth of real character!

Ampel.   I'm not some public picnic lunch!

---

[6] Although Plautus does not use a spoonerism, the English joke does bear some resemblance to the original. For the Plautine stock-in-trade, compare *Pseudolus,* lines 841–843.

Scepar. May I please squeeze you once, like this?
I'm fond of fondling pretty girls.   425

Ampel. When I have time, but only then,
I'll think of having fun with you;
Now, please help me with my errand:
Answer either yes or no.

Scepar. What do you want?

Ampel. (*pointing to her pitcher*) To a person of sense,
This piece of equipment reveals what I want.

Scepar. To a person of sense, this piece of equipment
Of mine reveals what I want, too.

Ampel. That Queen of Hearts from over there
Commanded me to fetch some water.   430

Scepar. Ah, but I'm the King:[7] if you
Don't grovel, you won't get a drop.
It took a lot to dig that well:
We toiled so hard with tools of steel;
Unless you coax me quite a lot,
You'll hardly steal it from me now.

Ampel. Why do you hold back a favor
Foreigners at war exchange?

Scepar. Why do you hold back a favor
Citizens at peace exchange?   435

Ampel. All right! No problem then, my darling,
I'll do everything you want.

Scepar. Hurray! How wonderful! I'm saved!
She's calling me her darling now.
The water's yours; your love won't go
In vain. Give me the jug.

---

[7] An apparent reference to gambling terms; the dice throw known as "The King" would beat the toss known as "Venus."

Ampel.	Here, take it.	
	Hurry and return it, please.	

Scepar. Wait here; I'll be right back, my darling. (*exit into house*)

Ampel. What am I going to tell the priestess,
Having loitered here so long?   440
(*As she waits nervously, she moves downstage.*)
I still feel miserable and frightened
Now, as I look out to sea.

Oh dear, what's that I see along the shore?   442–450[8]
My master the pimp and his Sicilian guest!
Oh dear, I thought they both were lost at sea.
More trouble's still alive than we supposed.
I'd better run inside and tell Palaestra;
We can take refuge at the altar here   455
Before this nasty pimp arrives to catch us.
                                                        (*exit into temple*)

Act II, Scene 5

Just as AMPELISCA *leaves the stage,* SCEPARNIO *reappears at the door of Daemones' cottage, almost delirious with delight. The pitcher that he carries obscures his vision.*

Scepar. Ye gods above! I never dreamed that water
Could be such fun: I just loved fetching it!
The well appeared far shallower than before.   460
The job's been effortless—touch wood!
Ain't I the rascal, falling in love today?

Here's your water, gorgeous. Here! I want you
To hold it this way, please, with dignity.
Where are you, darling? Water's here! Hey, you!   465
She loves me, I think. She's hiding, naughty girl.
Where are you? Will you take this jug? Hey, you!
All right, enough's enough. Seriously, though,

---

[8]At this point in the text, the traditional line numbering is confused; nothing is omitted in translation.

Will you take this jug? Where in the world are you?
I don't see her anywhere. She's making fun of me!   470
By Herc, I'll plunk it in the middle of the road.
But hang on! What if someone snatches it,
This sacred jug of Venus? I'd be in a mess.
Great Herc! I bet that woman's set a trap
To get me caught with Venus' sacred jug.   475
I mean, the judge would be quite right to let me
Rot in jail, if I'm seen holding this.
It's got letters: it can sing its owner's name!
By Herc, I'll ask the priestess to come out
And take this jug back. I'll approach the door.   480
Hey, Ptolemocratia! Come and get this jug of yours;
Some girl or other brought it to me here.
(*There is a moment of silence.*)
It'll have to be carried in. New job for me:
I must deliver water here as well. (*exit into temple*)

Act II, Scene 6

On the path from the shore (stage left), enter the pimp LABRAX, *wet and cranky. He is followed at a short distance by his Sicilian guest,* CHARMIDES, *an equally cantankerous old man.*

Labrax   Whoever wants a wretched beggar's life   485
            Should place his destiny in Neptune's hands:
            Get tangled up with him in any way,
            And home he'll send you, in a state like mine.
            Miss Liberty, I must say you were clever
            Not to put to sea with Hercules.[9]   490
            But where's that guest of mine who ruined me?
            He's coming!

Charm.   Labrax, what the hell's the rush?
            You're going so fast I can't keep up with you.

Labrax   I only wish, before I set eyes on you,
            You'd died a cruel death in Sicily.   495
            You brought this misery into my life.

---

[9]The mythological allusion is obscure.

Charm.   I only wish, that day you took me home,
        I'd found instead a quiet bed in jail!
        As long as you live, I pray to heaven that all
        The guests you entertain are just like you.   500

Labrax   I brought old lady Bad Luck home with me.
        I'm such an idiot, why did I listen to you?
        Why did I leave? Why climb aboard a ship?
        I lost more goods and chattels than I owned!

Charm.   I'm not surprised your vessel broke apart   505
        Beneath a crook and all his crooked spoils.

Labrax   You sank me with seductive promises.

Charm.   I dined upon a banquet fouler far
        Than Tereus' or Thyestes' fateful feast.[10]

Labrax   I'm done for! I feel sick! Please hold my head.   510

Charm.   By Pollux, I hope you vomit up your lungs.

Labrax   Ah, Palaestra and Ampelisca, where are you now?

Charm.   They're tasty fodder for the fish, I'd say.

Labrax   A beggar's life you offered; what a prize!
        I listened to your loud and empty lies.   515

Charm.   Display more gratitude; you really must!
        I got you drenched, and you'd been dry as dust.

Labrax   Aw, get away from me; go hang yourself!

Charm.   Exactly what I had in mind for you.

Labrax   Is any man more miserable than I?   520

Charm.   I'm far more miserable than you are, Labrax.

---

[10]Both these mythical Greek kings were tricked into eating their own children, Thyestes by his brother Atreus, and Tereus by his wife, Procne, and her sister Philomela (see note 14). The allusions have an unfortunate effect on Labrax's stomach.

Labrax	Why?

Charm.	I don't deserve my fate; you do.

(*Both are beginning to shiver uncontrollably.*)

Labrax	Dear bulrush, bulrush, sing thy praise on high; Thou keepst thyself so gloriously dry.[11]

Charm.	It's calisthenic practice time for me; That's why my words vibrate so jerkily.	525

Labrax	Your bath, dear Neptune, feels like melted ice: With clothes on, I'm still numb: it's not n-n-nice.

Charm.	No stall has he where warming drinks are sold. He serves a liquor salty and c-c-c-cold.	530

Labrax	How blissful is the blacksmith's blessed lot! He works near embers and is always hot.

Charm.	I wish I dried qu-quickly, like a duck, Who has a-qua-qua-quatic kind of luck.

Labrax	Should I take jobs on stage as Monster-Jaw?[12]	535

Charm.	Why you?

Labrax	Because my teeth go clickety-clack.

Charm.	I feel I'm c-c-c-cleaned out deservedly.

Labrax	How so?

Charm.	I d-d-d-dared to sail with you, Who turned the ocean upside down on me.

---

[11] Though its style marks this couplet as a tragic parody, its specific inspiration (if any) is unknown. In the shivering scene that follows, the Latin rhythmical evidence suggests that Plautus meant several lines to be delivered in a stammering chatter, including the duck quack that is reflected in the English translation.

[12] One of the comic stereotypes in the old Atellan farce was Manducus, a character with huge and scary movable jaws.

Labrax	I listened to you when you promised me	540
	That courtesans brought highest profits there;	
	You said that I could shovel in the cash.	

Charm. Did you expect, you filthy animal,
To gobble up the whole of Sicily?

Labrax	What huge sea monster gobbled up my trunk,	545
	Where all my gold and silver had been crammed?	

Charm. The same one, probably, that ate my wallet,
Full of cash, inside my haversack.

Labrax	Bah! I'm reduced to this confounded tunic	
	And this stupid cloak. I'm really through!	550

Charm. If you like, go into partnership with me:
We're down to equal shares.

Labrax   If only those
Young girls were safe, there'd still be some faint hope.
Now if the young man Plesidippus sees me,
After his down payment for Palaestra,   555
He'll create some trouble for me here.

Charm. Why cry, you boob? While you've a wagging tongue,
You're well supplied to pay off everyone.

Act II, Scene 7

Having delivered the pitcher, SCEPARNIO *now emerges from the temple. He does not immediately see* LABRAX *and* CHARMIDES.

Scepar.	What's going on, I'd like to know?	
	Why two young women inside the temple,	
	Crying, clinging to each other	
	And embracing Venus' statue,	560
	Frightened of someone and upset?	
	This very night, so they declare,	
	The two of them were shipwrecked and	
	Today the sea cast them ashore.	

250

| Labrax | By Herc, young man, I'd like to know, |
| | Where are those women that you speak of? |

| Scepar. | Here, in the temple of Venus. |

| Labrax | How many? |

| Scepar. | Exactly as many as you and I. |

| Labrax | They're doubtless mine? |

| Scepar. | I doubtless wouldn't know. |

| Labrax | What do they look like? |

Scepar.	Ravishing.	565
	I could fall in love with either,
	If I'd had enough to drink.

| Labrax | Doubtless young girls? |

| Scepar. | Doubtless you're |
| | A pain. Go see them, if you want. |

| Labrax | These girls inside here really must |
| | Be my young ladies, Charmides. |

| Charm. | Jupiter damn you, if they are, |
| | And damn you double, if they're not! |

| Labrax | I'll storm the shrine of Venus now. (*exit into temple*) |

Charm.	(*aside*) Too bad it's not the pit of hell.	570
	(*turning to address* SCEPARNIO)
	Good stranger, kindly let me know
	Where I can find some place to sleep.

| Scepar. | Sleep over there, wherever you want. |
| | No one will mind; it's public land. |

| Charm. | But surely you see how I'm dressed: |

My clothes are simply wringing wet.
Accompany me inside the house
And give me other clothes to wear
While mine are drying out; someday
I'll show my gratitude to you.   575

Scepar. That roof tile there is the one dry thing
I've got; you take it, if you want.[13]
It often serves me as a shawl
Or shelter from the pouring rain.
Give me your things: I'll see they get
Dried out.

Charm.   Hey! Isn't it enough
That I got badly soaked at sea?
Must I be squeezed out, here on shore?

Scepar. Whether you're soaked or squeezed or lathered
Couldn't matter less to me.   580
Never would I trust your word
Without a binding guarantee.
You can sweat or freeze to death,
Get sick, get better, I don't care.
I'm not keen to have some foreign
Stranger in our house. So there! (*exit into house*)

Charm. Has he gone now? He's had experience
Selling slaves, whoever he is;
He's merciless! But why am I standing
Here so wet and woebegone?   585
I ought to go inside the temple,
Where I can sleep away this jag
I got by drinking rather more
Than pleasure and good sense advised.
As though we were Greek wine-jugs, Neptune
Poured seawater into us,
Expecting that a dose of salts

---

[13]That Sceparnio is here referring to a roof tile (a deliciously comic image) was suggested by A. T. von S. Bradshaw, "Sceparnio's 'Raincoat' in Plautus, *Rudens* 576," *Classical Quarterly* 23 (1973): 275–278.

Would help to shake us up inside.
You get the point. If he had kept us
Partying a little longer,   590
We'd have fallen sound asleep:
He sent us homeward just in time.

    The pimp's inside; I'll check him out,
    My partner in that drinking bout. (*exit into temple*)

ACT III

No time has elapsed. Enter DAEMONES *from his cottage.*

Act III, Scene 1

Daemo.　It's strange the way the gods will tease mankind,
　　　　And strange the dreams they send us as we sleep:
　　　　Not even then are we allowed to rest.　　　　595
　　　　Take me, for instance. Just last night I had
　　　　A very strange and mystifying dream.

　　　　Beneath a swallow's nest, it seemed, an ape
　　　　Was mounting an attack, prepared to climb,
　　　　But couldn't reach the birds to snatch them. Then,　　600
　　　　It seems, the ape comes walking up to me,
　　　　And asks if I've a ladder I can lend.
　　　　In answer, I inform the ape that I'm
　　　　A native-born Athenian, and that swallows
　　　　Come from Athens—Philomela's girls.[14]
　　　　He mustn't hurt my dear compatriots.　　605
　　　　Well, now the creature's getting uglier;
　　　　He's threatening to do me dreadful harm.
　　　　He wants to sue me! Somehow, in a rage,
　　　　I seem to grab the ape around the middle,
　　　　Binding that obnoxious beast in chains.　　610

　　　　Now, what event this dream may signify
　　　　I've not been able yet to speculate.

---

[14]Philomela and her sister Procne, the ill-starred daughters of the Athenian king Pandion, were transformed into birds at the grisly climax of the myth of Tereus. I have adopted O. Skutsch's conjecture for amending this passage (*Classical Review* 16 [1966]: 12–14).

But what's that racket starting up next door
In Venus' temple? It's astonishing!

Act III, Scene 2

To the accompaniment of background noises from within, TRACHALIO *appears at the temple door, in a rhetorical frame of mind.*

Trach.   Good people of Cyrene,
    I beseech you, place your trust in me.   615
    You farmer fellows, country dwellers
    Now residing in these parts,
    Dear neighbors, help the helpless and
    Repel a most repulsive deed!
    Be instruments of vengeance! Don't let
    Wicked people wield more weight
    Than innocents who do not wish
    A notoriety from crime.
    Make shameless conduct stand condemned,
    Grant decency its just reward;   620
    Allow our lives to be controlled
    By law, not low brutality.
    Come running here to Venus' temple
    (I implore you once again),
    All of you present with me now
    And all who hear my urgent cry.
    Assist these suppliants who have placed
    Themselves, by custom old as time,
    In Venus' care and in the hands
    Of Venus' lady overseer.   625
    Seize injustice: wring its neck
    Before it can affect your lives.

Daemo.   What's all that fuss?

Trach.   By these old knees
    I call you to witness, aged sir,
    Whoever you are—

Daemo.   Let go my knees

And give me some idea why
You're causing this commotion here.

Trach. I beg and entreat you, if you hope
That you'll enjoy a bumper crop
Of asafetida this year,[15]   630
And that your export product will
Arrive in Capua safe and sound,
And (so may you always be
Immune to sore and runny eyes!)—

Daemo. You crazy?

Trach.   If you trust that you'll
Be raking in the silphium,
Don't hesitate, old sir, to give
The aid that I'll request of you.

Daemo. By your young back and legs and ankles,
I call you to witness, sir,   635
If you foresee a fertile crop,
A forestful of flogging sticks,
And hope this year that you'll enjoy
A harvest rich in punishment,
Just tell me what the problem is
And why you're making such a fuss.

Trach. Why be abusive? On my part,
I wished you nothing but the best.

Daemo. On mine, I speak you well, and pray
Events turn out as you deserve.   640

Trach. Then please turn your attention this way.

Daemo. What's the trouble?

Trach.   Two young women,

---

[15]The most famous product of Cyrene (which Trachalio assumes to be Daemones' crop, of course!) was the exotic plant silphium, known also as laserpicium, from which came the drug asafetida.

Innocent creatures, here inside
Most urgently require your help.
In violation of every law,
They underwent (still undergo!)
Flagrant abuse in Venus' shrine.
The temple priestess, what is more,
Is being treated shamefully.

Daemo. Who could have the effrontery   645
To dare a violent act against
A priestess? But those women, tell me:
Who are they? What harsh treatment have
They suffered?

Trach.   Listen; I'll explain.
They're clinging close to Venus' statue;
A man supremely arrogant
Would like to carry them away;
Both girls should actually be free.

Daemo. Who's the man who holds the gods
In such contempt?

Trach.   You want to know?   650
A fellow filled with foul deceit,
A crook, a liar, and a cheat;
A villain vile and unappealing,
Utterly devoid of feeling.
One word does it: *pimp*! Indeed,
What more description do you need?

Daemo. Holy Pollux, you describe
A man who should be soundly whipped.

Trach. He grabbed the priestess by the throat!   655

Daemo. By Herc, he did it at his peril!
Leave your stations, come outside,
Turbalio, Sparax! Where are you?[16]

---

[16] Although it is my policy not to anglicize significant names, I welcome John Fitch's suggestion that these two flogging-slaves could be called "Mayhem" and "Masher."

257

Trach.   Go in yourself and rescue them.

Daemo.   I'll not give the command again!

(*Enter* TURBALIO *and* SPARAX, *from Daemones' house.*)

Follow this way.

Trach.   Come on now, sir,
Order them to scoop his eyes,
Like cooks preparing cuttlefish!

Daemo.   Fling the scoundrel by his feet,
Exactly like a butchered pig!   660

(DAEMONES *and his two* SLAVES *disappear into the temple.*)

Trach.   I hear a ruckus. I believe
The pimp is getting raked with fists.
I hope they bash out every tooth
From his disreputable jaws!
But see the frightened girls themselves
Emerging from the temple here.

Act III, Scene 3

Enter PALAESTRA *and* AMPELISCA *from the temple, observed by* TRACHALIO.

Palaes.   Now is our moment of despair;
Helpless and defenseless
We are gripped by deprivation.   665
No direction anywhere;
Have we a pathway to salvation?
Both of us are filled with fear:
Our wicked, violent master
Ventured to manhandle us   670
Just now inside the temple here.
He pushed the aged priestess
Backward, forward (scandalous!),
And dragged us from the holy statue

	By sheer might.	
	The way our fortunes stand at present,	
	Dying is right;	675
	No act is preferable to death	
	In times of misery and fright.	

Trach.   What is it? Who can that be speaking?
Do I hesitate to comfort them?
Palaestra!

Palaes.   Who is calling?

Trach.   Ampelisca!

Ampel.   Please, who's calling?

Palaes.   Who's addressing us by name?

Trach.   Look around and you will know.

Palaes.   O hope of my salvation!

Trach.   Be quiet and keep your courage up.   680
Trust me!

Palaes.   If only we may be allowed
Not to be crushed by violence:
Violence that forces me
To inflict violence on myself.

Trach.   Enough! You're being foolish.

Palaes.   Stop trying to console me now
In my misery with words alone;
Unless you offer real help,
Trachalio, our game is up.

Ampel.   I'm resolved to meet my death
Before I let this pimp get me.
And yet I have a woman's heart:
When I envision the dire deed,   685

My limbs are loosened in despair.
Dear Pollux, what a bitter day!

Trach.   Keep up your courage.

Palaes.   All right, tell me:
Where's that courage to be found?

Trach.   Don't be afraid, you two; sit down
Here, at the altar.

Ampel.   How can that altar
Give us more secure support
Than Venus' statue in the shrine?
Just now we clung to it, but then
Were cruelly removed by force.   690

Trach.   Sit down right here, and I'll protect you
From this side. Regard the altar
As your encampment and your ramparts;
I'll be your defensive line.
With Venus watching over us,
I'll march against the wicked pimp!

Palaes.   We do as you ask us.
                    Gentle Venus,
Both of us implore you as we
Clasp our arms around your altar,
Weeping, falling on our knees: 695
Receive us in your tender care,
Protect us and watch over us.
Take vengeance on those wicked men
Who held your temple in contempt,
And, with your blessing, suffer us
To occupy this altar here.
We both have been well washed and rinsed
By Neptune's efforts in the night,
And so you mustn't take offense
Or find the two of us at fault,   700
If you consider anything
To be less laundered than you like.

Trach. These girls' request is fair, I say;
     Do let them, Venus, have their way.
     To pardon them is only right,
     Since they've been driven here by fright.
     If a mussel shell created you,
     Don't scorn them: they've got mussels, too.[17]

     Good timing, look! The old man's here:
     An advocate for all of us.   705

Act III, Scene 4

Enter DAEMONES *from the temple, as his two burly slaves* TURBALIO *and* SPARAX *drag out* LABRAX. *The young* WOMEN *continue to huddle in their place of refuge at the altar.*

Daemo. Come out of the temple, most profane
     Of all men ever born on earth!
     You women, sit down by the altar.
     Where have they gone to?

Trach.   Look this way.

Daemo. That's excellent; as we had hoped.
     Just tell the fellow to approach.
     (*to* LABRAX) Do you suppose the gods approve
     Of your unlawful actions here?
     (*to a* SLAVE) Fling a fist in his face!

Labrax   Unfair!
     Unjust! You'll pay for this.   710

Daemo. Can he be threatening? What nerve!

Labrax My legal rights have been removed;
     You're snatching my two female slaves,
     Against my will.

---

[17]There is a sexual double entendre in Trachalio's use of the Latin word *concha*. The birth of Venus from a seashell was a familiar image in ancient painting.

Trach.	Get an arbitrator,
	Some fine plutocratic fellow
	From the senate of Cyrene,
	To rule on whether these girls are yours,
	Or whether they shouldn't go free instead,
	Or whether it isn't really right
	That you should now be jammed in jail,
	To live forever and a day,
	Pacing the prison floor away.

Trach.   Get an arbitrator,
Some fine plutocratic fellow
From the senate of Cyrene,
To rule on whether these girls are yours,
Or whether they shouldn't go free instead,
Or whether it isn't really right
That you should now be jammed in jail,   715
To live forever and a day,
Pacing the prison floor away.

Labrax I didn't get out of bed today
To gossip with a gallows bird.
(*to* DAEMONES) It's you I'm naming.

Daemo.   Handle him first
In your dispute; he knows you best.

Labrax I'm dealing with you.

Trach.   But you must deal
With me. Are those slave women yours?

Labrax They are.

Trach.   Very well. Touch either one
With a tiny little finger tip.   720

Labrax And if I do?

Trach.   By Herc, at once
I'll turn you into a punching bag:
I'll suspend you in the air
And pound you to pieces, perjured pimp!

Labrax May I be allowed to take
My girls away from Venus' altar?

Daemo. No, you may not; we have a law
On that.

Labrax   I'll have no truck or trade

With your laws. Now it's my intent
To take the two of them away.   725
If you're in love with them, old man,
We'll need to have some cold cash;
If they've attracted Venus' eye,
Then she can keep them—for a price.

Daemo. The gods pay you? Now listen here,
I'll let you know the way I feel:
Begin to push these girls around
Even a smidgen, as a joke,
And I'll dismiss you in such a state
That you won't recognize yourself.   730
(*to his* SLAVES) You fellows: when I give the sign,
If you don't bash his eyeballs out,
My whips will bind you round about
As rushes wrap up myrtle sprays.

Labrax That's force: illegal!

Trach.   You accusing
Us of force, you blazing blackguard?

Labrax You great, grand son of a bitch, where do you
Get the nerve to be so rude?

Trach. Fine! I'm a great, grand son of a bitch,
And you're a perfect gentleman: 735
Is that less reason for these ladies
To be free?

Labrax   They're free, you claim?

Trach. And your superiors, too, by Herc!
And what is more, authentic Greeks;
This one's Athenian born and bred,
Of freeborn native parentage.

Daemo. What's this I hear you say?

Trach. That she was born in Athens, free.

Daemo.	Can she be my compatriot?	
Trach.	Cyrene's not your birthplace, then?	740

Daemo. No, no! Athens, in Attica.
Born and reared and schooled right there.

Trach. Old sir, I beg you, do protect
Your countrywomen.

Daemo.   (*aside*) Oh, my daughter!
Though far off, you call to mind
My sorrows, when I see this girl.
The three-year-old I lost would now
Be just this big, if she's alive.

Labrax I gave good cash for both these two,   745
And paid their owner personally.
What difference does it make if they
Were born in Athens or in Thebes,
Provided they deserve to serve
As slaves of mine?

Trach.   Shame on you!
Are you some prowling alley cat,
To pounce on innocent young children
Who've been kidnapped from their parents,
Grinding them in a foul trade?

As for the second girl, though I
Don't know her nationality,   750
I'm sure she's far more virtuous
Than you, you masterpiece of slime.

Labrax No worse than you!

Trach.   Let's have a contest:
Who's got the more truthful back?
If you don't show more seamy patches,
More repair marks down your spine
Than any battleship has nails,

Then I'm the greatest liar here.
After I've inspected your back,
You can take a peek at mine: 755
If you don't find it so unmarked
That any leather-worker would
Pronounce it perfect for a job
(An absolutely flawless hide!),
What reason is there why I shouldn't
Flail and flog you till I'm tired?

Why are you staring at the girls?
You touch them and I'll knock your eyes out!

Labrax   All right, since you forbid me now
To carry either girl away—   760

Daemo.   What will you do?

Labrax   I'll bring in Vulcan,
Venus' fiery enemy.
(*He moves toward the door of Daemones' cottage.*)

Trach.   Where's he going?

Labrax   Hey, anyone home here?
Hey!

Daemo.   The moment you touch that door,
I'll make a *hey*-stack of your face
With my two-fisted pitchfork here.

Sparax   We don't keep any fire on hand;
Dried figs provide our only food.

Trach.   I'll give you fire, if there's a chance
I can ignite it on your noggin.   765

Labrax   By Herc, I'm going somewhere else
To look for fire.

Daemo.   And when it's found?

Labrax	I'm going to light a scorcher here.
Daemo.	To singe out all your sinfulness?
Labrax	No, no. To burn them both alive On the altar here, that's what I want.
Trach.	By Herc! I'll straightway grab your beard And flip you on that flaming fire, Then fling you out, a half-cooked roast, For nasty birds to nibble on.

770

Daemo.	(*aside*) As I mull the matter over, I've been thinking: that's the ape Who wanted to remove these swallows From their nest, against my will, Just as I dreamt it in my sleep.
Trach.	You know what I ask of you, old sir? To guard them and ward off violence Until I bring my master back.
Daemo.	Go look for your master; bring him here.
Trach.	Don't let this man—
Daemo.	He'll rue the day He touches them or even tries!

775

Trach.	Take care.
Daemo.	It has been taken. Go!
Trach.	Guard him, too; he mustn't escape. We've promised the executioner Either a silver talent or The fellow in the flesh, today.
Daemo.	Go on, I'll look after all this Properly.
Trach.	I'll soon be back. (*exit stage left*)

Act III, Scene 5

LABRAX *is still offering some resistance to Daemones' slaves,* TURBALIO *and* SPARAX. *The silent figures of* PALAESTRA *and* AMPELISCA *continue to occupy the altar.*

Daemo. Would you prefer, dear pimp, if you had the choice,   780
       To calm down with a drubbing or without?

Labrax I don't give a hoot for what you say, old man.
       Though you and Venus and Jove all disapprove,
       I'll snatch my women by the hair!

Daemo.   Just try!

Labrax I'll try all right.

Daemo.   Come on, just move this way.   785

Labrax Then tell those boys of yours to move aside.

Daemo. No, they'll move up.

Labrax   By Herc, I don't approve.

Daemo. If they move forward, what'll you do?

Labrax   Back off.
       The next time I run into you in town,
       Old man, let no one call me "pimp" again   790
       If I don't make a mockery of you.

Daemo. Do carry out those threats of yours; meanwhile,
       You touch the girls, you get a wicked whack.

Labrax How wicked?

Daemo.   Well designed to match a pimp.

Labrax Your menaces don't mean a thing to me;   795
       Despite you, I'll still grab these two.

Daemo. Just touch them!

Labrax Well, I will!

Daemo. At what cost, do you know?
Go now, Turbalio, on the run, and fetch
Two cudgels.

Labrax Cudgels?

Daemo. Good ones. Make it quick.

(TURBALIO *enters the house.*)

(*to* LABRAX) You'll get the warm reception you deserve. 800

Labrax (*aside*) "Alas! I lost my helm at sea, poor me!"[18]
To have a helmet would be handy now.
(*to* DAEMONES) May I at least call out to them?

Daemo. No, sir!
Ha! Look! Sweet Pollux, the cudgel boy is back. 805

(TURBALIO *returns from the house with two clubs.*)

Labrax Sweet Pollux, I've a tingling in my ears.

Daemo. Come on, take one of the cudgels from him, Sparax.
You stand on this side, Turbalio over here.
Positions, both! That's good. Now get this straight:
If he lays one unwelcome finger on them, 810
And you don't make him welcome to the club,
So welcome he'll have trouble getting home,
You both are through! If he calls out to them,
Reply from where you're standing, in their stead.
And if he's keen to get away, be quick 815
To stroke his lovely legs with cudgel blows.

Labrax You mean that I can't leave?

---

[18]This verse appears to be either a proverbial expression or a tragic parody.

Daemo.   I've said enough.
And when that slave returns here with his boss
(The man he went to find), go home at once.
Look after this assignment with great care.   820
                          (*exit into house*)

Labrax   Dear Herc! That temple's quickly been transformed:
From Venus it has passed to Hercules—
The old boy's put two statues here with clubs.
By Herc, I don't know where on earth to run,
Since land and sea both rage against me now.   825
Palaestra!

Turbal.   What do you want?

Labrax   There's something wrong;
For this Palaestra speaking isn't mine.
Ampelisca, hey!

Sparax   Beware of punishment!

Labrax   (*aside*) Within their limits, they offer good advice.
(*aloud*) I'm speaking to you. You girls! Do you object   830
If I come closer to them?

Slaves   No, we don't mind.

Labrax   Will I be in trouble?

Turbal.   Not if you watch out.

Labrax   Watch out for what?

Turbal.   Enormous punishment.

Labrax   Aw, Herc! Just let me leave!

Sparax   Leave if you want.

Labrax   Oh, excellent! I'm grateful to you both.   835

(*The two* SLAVES *suddenly block his path.*)

I think I'd rather not.

Slaves   Stay where you are.

Labrax   I've come off terribly in many ways.
I'm now resolved to starve these women out.

Act III, Scene 6

Having found his master, TRACHALIO *returns with* PLESIDIPPUS, *stage left. They converse for some moments before moving within sight of* LABRAX, *his* GUARDS, *and the two* GIRLS.

Plesid.   That villain wished to visit violence
Upon my girl, at Venus' altar?

Trach.   That's correct.   840

Plesid.   Why didn't you kill him on the spot?

Trach.   No sword.

Plesid.   You could have grabbed a club or stone.

Trach.   What, chase
A man with stones, just like a dog? Bad form.

Labrax   (*aside*) Oh, Pollux! Plesidippus! Here! I'm doomed.
He'll sweep me up, to the final speck of dust.   845

Plesid.   Were the women sitting at the altar then,
When you came to get me?

Trach.   Yes, and still there now.

Plesid.   Who's guarding them at present?

Trach.   Some old fellow,
Venus' neighbor, working with a will.

| | He's flanked by flunkies now; I gave the word. | 850 |

He's flanked by flunkies now; I gave the word.   850

Plesid.   Take me straight to the pimp. Where is that man?

Labrax   Hello.

Plesid.   To hell with your hello's! Think fast:
Would you rather be knotted by the neck, or dragged?
While time permits, choose either.

Labrax   Neither, please.

Plesid.   Go down to the shore on the run, Trachalio.   855
Instruct my friends to meet me at the harbor,
The ones I brought to get this fellow hanged.
Come back here then and take a turn on guard.
I'll drag this crook to court—or send him packing.

(*As* TRACHALIO *leaves for the shore, stage left,* PLESIDIPPUS *turns to*
LABRAX.)

To court! Let's walk!

Labrax   What wrong have I done?

Plesid.   You ask?   860
You who took my deposit on a girl
And stole her away?

Labrax   Not really true.

Plesid.   Why not?

Labrax   Our ship got *off*; it couldn't get *away*.
I said that I'd present myself at Venus'
Shrine. Have I reneged? Am I not there?   865

Plesid.   Save it for court; one word's enough for now:
Follow!

Labrax   Charmides, rescue me, I beg!
He's got me by the neck!

Rudens

(*Enter* CHARMIDES *through the temple door.*)

Charm.   Who calls my name?

Labrax   See how I'm being snatched?

Charm.   I'm glad to see it.

Labrax   Will you not rescue me?

Charm.   Who's snatching you?   870

Labrax   Young Plesidippus.

Charm.   Reap as ye have sown!
You'd better crawl to your lockup with a smile.
You have achieved what most men dream about.

Labrax   What's that?

Charm.   To reach at last their lifelong goal.

Labrax   Follow me, please!

Charm.   Your counsel's like your character: 875
You're off to the lockup, so you'd have me follow.

Plesid.   Still hanging on?

Labrax   I'm done for.

Plesid.   Wouldn't I like!
My dear Palaestra and Ampelisca, wait
Right here till I return.

Turbal.   I recommend
They stay at our house until then.

Plesid.   All right,   880
You're gracious friends.

Labrax   I'd say you're thugs.

Turbal.   Thugs? Grab him!

(SPARAX *quickly subdues* LABRAX, *and the two* SLAVES *escort* PALAES-
TRA *and* AMPELISCA *into Daemones' cottage.*)

Labrax   Please, Palaestra! Save me!

Plesid.   Come, you scum!

Labrax   My guest—

Charm.   Not guest: I'm swearing off that role.

Labrax   You spurn me like this?

Charm.   I do. One drink's enough.

Labrax   May heaven plague you!

Charm.   *You* deserve that blessing.   885

(PLESIDIPPUS *and* LABRAX *leave for town, stage right.* CHARMIDES
speaks directly to the audience.)

Men do get transformed into animals,
I think; that pimp's become a jailbird now.
He'll soon be in a flap inside the coop,
As he prepares to nest in lockup-land.

But still, I'll back him up in court today;   890
With my help, he'll be quickly—put away.

ACT IV

It is the same morning. Enter DAEMONES *from his cottage. He speaks directly to the audience.*

Act IV, Scene 1

Daemo.   My good deed for the day! I'm pleased that I
Could help these girls. I've found new protégées:
Two lovely little ladies, dear young things.
My wretched wife is always watching me,   895
In case I even glance at pretty girls.

But our slave Gripus—I wonder what he's up to?
He went out to sea last night to fish.
He'd have been smarter to have slept at home:
His efforts and his nets are just a farce,   900
The way the weather's been last night and now.
I'll fry on my fingers all he caught today,
To judge from those wild breakers bashing in.

My wife is calling me to lunch. I'm off.
She'll fill my ears with idiotic chatter.   905
                                          (*exit into house*)

Act IV, Scene 2

Enter from the shore, stage left, Daemones' slave GRIPUS, *who returns from his expedition dragging his fishing net, in which he has snared a small wickerwork trunk. A soggy rope trails behind his net. As he labors, he sings exultantly.*

Gripus   All thanks be to Neptune, my lord and protector,

Whose kingdom is briny and teeming with fishes,
Where I've been discharged in magnificent fashion,
All laden with loot! My return is auspicious:
My dory is safe from the blustery ocean,   910
Its catch looking wonderfully strange and delicious.

This most amazing haul's the nicest
Stroke of luck I've ever met;
I didn't catch an ounce of fish,
But look what I've got in my net!

Last night I eagerly arose,   915
Preferring profit to repose;
Although the storm was fierce outside,
I spared no effort as I tried
To ease my master's poverty
And struggle for my liberty.

I can't abide a lazy man;
That type of conduct seems a crime.   920
A person should be wide awake
Who wants to finish work on time.
To lie around until your master
Gets you going: that's not proper!
Men who only like to sleep
Run short of cash and come a cropper.

By putting laziness aside,
I now have found what may provide
    A life of ease
    If I should please:
This object that the sea's supplied.   925
    The thing I've caught
    Weighs quite a lot,
Whatever it has got inside.

There's gold in here: there has to be;
And no one knows of it but me!

Now Gripus, here's a chance for you
To win your freedom right away.

Now here's my method, here's my plan.
I'll cunningly approach my boss
And bargain with him, little by little,
Pledging cash for liberty.
And when I'm free—well, then, of course   930
I'll heap up houses, land, and slaves;
I'll ply my trade with mighty ships,
And be accounted king of kings.
I'll build myself a pleasure craft
And copy Stratonicus' way
Of making tours around the world.[19]
And when my fame is at its peak,
I'll build a grand community;
I'll call that city "Gripusburg,"
A monument to my renown   935
And center of my mighty realm.
I'm contemplating mighty deeds!

But now I'll put away this trunk.
Today My Majesty will have to dine
On salt and vinegar, not meat and wine.

Act IV, Scene 3

Having paused in his task of dragging the net, GRIPUS *now resumes his labor and moves in the direction of Daemones' cottage.* TRACHALIO *enters, stage left, returning from his errand to the shore; he overtakes* GRIPUS, *seizes the rope, and gives it a jerk.*

Trach.   Hey, wait!

Gripus   Why should I wait?

Trach.   So I
         Can coil this rope you're trailing here.

---

[19]Stratonicus was a celebrated fourth-century musician, still well remembered when Diphilus wrote the Greek original of *Rudens*. Plautus perhaps misunderstood the reference and imagined Stratonicus to be a great Hellenistic king. See W. S. Anderson, "Gripus and Stratonicus," *American Journal of Philology* 107 (1986): 560–563.

Gripus	Let go!

Trach.   But look, I'm helping you.
"Good deeds to the good go not in vain."

Gripus We had a wild storm yesterday.   940
I haven't any fish, young man,
So don't imagine that I do.
Can't you see my dripping net
Is "destitute of scaly flock"?

Trach. Dear Pollux! I don't want your fish;
I'm hungry for your conversation.

Gripus You bore me to death, whoever you are.

Trach. Well, I won't let you leave here. Stay!

Gripus Watch out for trouble! Why the hell
Are you pulling back against me?

Trach.   Listen!   945

Gripus I'm not listening.

Trach.   But you'll have to,
Someday.

Gripus   All right, speak your piece.

Trach. The story that I've got to tell
Is certainly worth listening to.

Gripus Oh, come on, get it out.

Trach.   Make sure
That no one's hovering nearby.

Gripus Has it anything to do with me?

Trach. Of course. May I count on your discretion?   950

Gripus   Just tell me what it all means!

Trach.   Shh!
I'll tell you, if you pledge good faith
That you'll not treat me faithlessly.

Gripus   I pledge good faith that I'll be faithful,
Whoever you are.

Trach.   Then listen.   955
I saw a man commit a theft;
I knew the owner, now bereft.
I met the robber, by and by,
And made this offer to the guy:
"I know the victim of your deed.
One-half the loot is what I need;
My silence will be guaranteed."
The thief said nothing in reply.
You tell me: what's my proper share?   960
One-half?

Gripus   No! Even more is fair!
Inform the owner, otherwise.

Trach.   All right, I'll do as you advise.
Now pay attention; all of this
Pertains to you.

Gripus   Exactly how?

Trach.   For a long time I have known the man
To whom that trunk belongs.

Gripus   You have?

Trach.   And I know how the trunk got lost.

Gripus   But I know how the trunk got found;
I also know the man who found it,
And the present owner, too.   965
My secret isn't any more

Your business than yours is mine;
For I know whose it is right now,
And you know whose it was back when.
Nobody's going to get this trunk,
So don't be hoping that you can.

Trach. Not even the owner, if he showed up?

Gripus Make no mistake, the owner is
No son of mother born but me.
I caught it on my fishing trip.   970

Trach. Oh, really?

Gripus   Will you admit that any
Fish out there at sea are mine?
The ones I happen to catch belong
To me; I treat them as my own.
No one asserts his right to them
Or even makes a partial claim.
Down in the forum, openly,
I sell them all as my own wares.
Beyond a doubt, the sea is common
To everyone.

Trach.   Oh, I agree.   975
But how's it right, then, that this trunk
Is not my common property?
It turned up in the common sea.

Gripus Haven't you a shred of shame?
If your position became law,
Fishermen would be gone for good.
The instant any fish got put out
In the marketplace for sale,
No one would buy: each person would
Demand his individual share   980
Of produce from the common sea.

Trach. You cheeky man, what are you saying?
Have you the unmitigated gall

> To compare a trunk with fish?
> Do the objects seem the same?

Gripus   The question's out of my control;
When I have lowered my net or hook,
I pull out everything that sticks.
Whatever net or hook can catch
Belongs to me, emphatically!   985

Trach.   By Herc, it doesn't! Not if you
Remove a man-made object.

Gripus   Quibbler!

Trach.   Look, you drop of poison, have you
Ever known a fisherman
To actually land a trunk-fish
Or display one in the market?
You're not going to hold down every
Occupation that you want:
You low-life, you expect to be
Both basket boy and fisherman.   990
You must either show me that
A fish can be a wicker trunk
Or else abandon anything
Not sea-produced or scaly-clad.

Gripus   But have you never heard before?
The trunk-fish does exist.

Trach.   You crook!
There's no such thing.

Gripus   Oh yes, there is.
I know, and I'm a fisherman.
It's seldom caught; no fish that swims
Will come less often to the land.   995

Trach.   That's nonsense! You just hope that you
Can hoodwink me, you gallows bird.

Gripus   Only teeny-weeny ones

Are caught the color we've got here.
Others have got scarlet skin—
Big fellows; black ones, too.

Trach.   Indeed.
By Herc! I think if you're not careful,
You'll be turning trunk-fish twice:
Your skin will first be beaten scarlet,
Getting blacker later on.   1000

Gripus   (*aside*) What a crook I've met today!

Trach.   While we are talking, time's a-wasting.
Who do you think should arbitrate
And settle our dispute?

Gripus   I'd like
Judge Trunk.

Trach.   Judge Trunk?

Gripus   That's right.

Trach.   You fool!

Gripus   Well, Doctor Thales, I presume!

Trach.   You'll not receive this trunk today
Unless you name an arbitrator
Or trustee to act as judge
In our dispute.

Gripus   Are you quite sane?   1005

Trach.   I'm raving mad.

Gripus   Well, I'm possessed,
But won't let go in any case.

Trach.   Just speak another word, and bang!
I'll hide my fist inside your brain.
If you don't soon release your hold,

> I'll handle you like some new sponge
> Receiving its first squeeze, and squish out
> All the juice you've got inside.

Gripus   Touch me, and I'll dash you to the ground
          The way I treat an octopus.   1010
          You want to fight?

Trach.   Whatever for?
          Why not divide the loot instead?

Gripus   Apart from trouble, you can't get
          A thing from me, so don't expect it.
          I'm leaving this way.

(*With the two men still clutching opposite ends of the net,* GRIPUS *starts to pull it toward Daemones' cottage.* TRACHALIO *moves ahead to cut him off.*)

Trach.   I'll swing the ship
          Around this way, so you can't leave. Wait!

Gripus   If you're the lookout in the bow,
          I'll be the helmsman in the stern.
          Release the rope, you criminal!

Trach.   I will, if you release the trunk.   1015

Gripus   I swear to Herc you'll not leave here
          So much as a single scrap the richer.

Trach.   You can't prevail on me by always
          Saying no; I'll need my share,
          Or else it's arbitration time,
          Or this goes under lock and key.

Gripus   You mean, what I caught in the sea?

Trach.   And I eye-witnessed from the shore.

Gripus   My effort, labor, net, and boat?

Trach.	If the owner came along right now,	1020
	Wouldn't I, who from a distance	
	Witnessed you obtaining this,	
	Be thought no less a thief than you?	

Gripus   No less.

Trach.   Aha! You whipping-post:
By what logic am I a thief
And not your partner? Tell me that!

Gripus   I don't know a thing about
Your complicated city laws;
I only know that this is mine.

Trach.   And likewise, I declare it's mine.   1025

Gripus   Wait! I think I've found a way
You can be neither thief nor partner.

Trach.   What way?

Gripus   Let me leave from here,
While you leave quietly yourself.
Don't give me away to anyone;
I won't give anything to you.
If you keep quiet, I'll keep mum:
This is the best and fairest plan.

Trach.   Have you some offer you'd like to make?

Gripus   Well, that's what I've been doing now: 1030
Just go away, let go the rope,
And most of all, don't bother me.

Trach.   Wait; I'll make my counteroffer.

Gripus   Make yourself invisible!

Trach.   Do you know anyone in these parts?

Gripus   I ought to; this is my neighborhood.

Trach.   Where do you live round here?

Gripus   Far off . . .
           Over there . . . way out in the fields.

Trach.   Do you want our case to be considered
           By the man who lives right here?   1035

Gripus   Slacken the rope a little, while
           I step aside and ponder that.

Trach.   All right.

Gripus   (*aside*) Ho, ho! Success!
           This loot is mine forever now.
           He wants my master to arbitrate
           My case inside my own backyard!
           By Herc, he'll never award a penny
           Penalty against his own.
           This fellow doesn't know the terms
           He set. I'll go to arbitration.   1040

Trach.   Well?

Gripus   Although I know for sure
           This trunk's my rightful property,
           I'll do as you suggest, instead
           Of fighting with you.

Trach.   Now you're talking!

Gripus   You drive me to an unknown judge.
           If he exhibits honesty
           I'll know the man; but otherwise,
           A known judge I'd not recognize.

                    Act IV, Scene 4

As GRIPUS *and* TRACHALIO *approach the cottage door, suddenly it opens, and*

DAEMONES *emerges in confusion, accompanied by* PALAESTRA, AMPELISCA, *and the two slaves* TURBALIO *and* SPARAX.

Daemo. Great Pollux! Seriously, ladies,
Though I'm entirely on your side,   1045
I am afraid my wife may drive me
Out of the house on your account.
Two concubines, she'll say, I've brought
Back home before her very eyes.
Escape to the altar there before
I have to.

Women   We're lost! What misery!

Daemo. I'll keep you safe, don't be afraid.
(*to* SLAVES) Why have you followed me outside
The house? As long as I'm around,
No one will do them any harm.   1050
Go inside now, both of you.
Guards! To the garrison: dismissed!

(*The* SLAVES *return to the house.*)

Gripus Master, good day.

Daemo.   Good day, Gripus.
How are you doing?

Trach.   He's your slave?

Gripus And proud of it.

Trach.   I'm not talking to you.

Gripus Then go away.

Trach.   Please answer, sir:
Is he your slave?

Daemo.   He's mine.

Trach.   Oh, that's

Just excellent, if he is yours.
Well met again.

Daemo.   The same to you.
Are you the one who went away   1055
A while ago to fetch his master?

Trach.   I'm the one.

Daemo.   What now do you want?

Trach.   This fellow's really yours?

Daemo.   He's mine.

Trach.   It's excellent that he's your slave.

Daemo.   What's the trouble?

Trach.   He's a villain,
That man there.

Daemo.   What did this villain
Do to you?

Trach.   I'd like to crack
The wretched fellow's anklebones.

Daemo.   What is it? Why are you having
This dispute, you two?

Trach.   I will explain.   1060

Gripus   No, I'll explain.

Trach.   I've got the floor,
I do believe.

Gripus   If you could feel
Ashamed, you'd leave the floor alone.

Daemo.   Gripus, shape up and pipe down.

Gripus	So he can be the first to speak?
Daemo.	Just listen! (*to* TRACHALIO) Speak!
Gripus	You'll let a stranger Make a speech ahead of me?
Trach.	The man's impossible to silence! As I was starting out to say, That pimp you shoved outside the temple 1065 Just a little while ago— This fellow has his trunk. Look there!
Gripus	I haven't.
Trach.	Do you deny what's plain To see?
Gripus	I wish you'd see much less. I have it, I haven't: what's the fuss About my personal affairs?
Trach.	How you got it matters a lot. Did you have justice on your side?
Gripus	If I didn't catch it, there's no reason I should not be crucified. 1070 If I caught it in my net at sea, How is it yours instead of mine?
Trach.	He's spinning a tale. It all took place As I'm describing.
Gripus	What are you saying?
Trach.	(*to* DAEMONES) What any respectable man would say: Stuff this fellow, if he's yours.
Gripus	Hey! You want it done to me The way your master jumps on you? Though he may like to "stuff" his slaves, Our master doesn't act that way. 1075

Daemo.	He beat you in that exchange, at least. What do you want now? Let me know.
Trach.	I'm not requesting any portion Of that trunk as my own share, Nor have I ever claimed it's mine; But there's a little box inside Belonging to this woman, who, As I have stated, should be free.
Daemo.	I assume you mean the girl You said was my compatriot?
Trach.	Exactly; and those trinkets that She wore when she was just a child Are there inside the little box, Which is, in turn, inside the trunk. The object's useless to your man, And will relieve her misery— If he gives her what she needs to find Her parents.
Daemo.	I'll make him give it. (*to* GRIPUS) Hush!
Gripus	By Herc, I'm going to give him nothing!
Trach.	Nothing do I ask except The box and trinkets.
Gripus	What if they're gold?
Trach.	What difference will it make to you? Gold will be redeemed with gold, And silver paid in silver weight.
Gripus	Please, I'd like to see your gold Before I let you see the chest.
Daemo.	(*to* GRIPUS) Watch out for trouble and shut up! (*to* TRACHALIO) Continue as you have begun.
Trach.	I ask one favor only: be

1080

1085

	Compassionate toward this woman,	1090
	If indeed this trunk belongs	
	To the pimp, as I suspect it does;	
	Without conclusive proof as yet,	
	I state it on conjecture.	

Gripus You see? The crook has set a trap.

Trach. Allow me to finish what I'm saying.
If in fact the trunk belongs
To the criminal I've spoken of,
These girls will be able to recognize it.
Make him show it to them.

Gripus   Show it?   1095

Daemo. It's quite a fair suggestion, Gripus,
That the girls be shown the trunk.

Gripus By Herc, it's not! It's notably unfair!

Daemo. Why?

Gripus   Because, if I show it to them,
Immediately, of course, they'll say
They recognize it.

Trach.   Nasty man!
Do you think everyone's the same
As you, you prince of perjury?

Gripus I'll bear all your abuse with ease,
As long as master's on my side.   1100

Trach. He may be standing on your side;
He'll draw his evidence from us.

Daemo. Shape up, Gripus! (*to* TRACHALIO) Sir, be brief.
Explain to us what you require.

Trach. I did explain, but if you haven't
Understood, I'll speak again.

These women, as I said before,
Should both enjoy their liberty.
This one was kidnapped, when she was
A little girl in Athens.

Gripus   Tell me,   1105
How does it affect my trunk
If these two girls are slaves or free?

Trach.   You want me to repeat it all,
You swine, to waste the time of day.

Daemo.   Control your vulgar language and
Conclude your explanation, please.

Trach.   Inside that trunk there ought to be
A tiny little wicker box
Containing signs that would allow
This girl to prove her parentage.   1110
She had them with her when, as a child,
She vanished from Athens, as I've said.

Gripus   May Jove and every god damn you!
What are you saying, tattle-tongue?
Are these girls deaf and dumb, that they
Can't do the talking for themselves?

Trach.   They're quiet: a woman's worth is always
Judged by silence, not by speech.

Gripus   Then you're without your proper share
Of man or woman, I believe.   1115

Trach.   How so?

Gripus   Because you're always worthless:
Silent, speaking, either way.
(*to* DAEMONES) Please, will I never be allowed
To speak today?

Daemo.   Hereafter, if

You utter a solitary word,
I'll crumple in your cranium.

Trach. As I began to say, old sir,
I urge you to instruct your man
To hand the little box to these girls.
If he demands some payment for it   1120
In return, oblige him: let him
Keep whatever else is there.

Gripus Now at last you're saying this,
Because you know it's rightly mine.
Before, you were aiming to go halves.

Trach. And afterwards it's still my aim.

Gripus I've seen a hungry kite take aim
And yet fly off with empty claws.

Daemo. Can't I shut you up without
An act of violence?

Gripus   If he's quiet,   1125
I'll be quiet; if he speaks,
Then let me give my side of things.

Daemo. Gripus, hand that trunk to me.

Gripus I'll trust you with it, on this one
Condition: if that stuff's not there,
I get it back.

Daemo.   Agreed.

Gripus   Then here.

(GRIPUS *lifts the trunk from the net, and passes it to* DAEMONES.)

Daemo. Palaestra! You too, Ampelisca.
Listen now to what I say.
(*to* PALAESTRA) Is this the trunk that you have said
Contains your little box?

Palaes.	It is.	1130

Gripus   Holy Herc, I'm dead and buried!
Even before she got a look
She said it was the same!

Palaes.   I'll get
This business back on level ground.

Inside that trunk there ought to be
A tiny little wicker box.
I shall identify its contents,
Naming each of them in turn.
Don't show me any object. If
I'm wrong, my words will be in vain,   1135
And you can keep whatever items
You have found inside the trunk.
But if I'm right, I beg that my
Possessions be returned to me.

Daemo.   I concur. That's merely just,
In my opinion.

Gripus   Not in mine!
What if she's a psychic or
A fortune-teller, and can know
For certain everything inside?
Will a fortune-teller get it?   1140

Daemo.   She'll get it if she tells the truth:
Psychic powers will do no good.
(*to* GRIPUS) Untie the trunk and let me know
The truth as soon as possible.

Trach.   He's had it!

Gripus   It's untied.

Daemo.   Then open it!

Palaes.   I see the box.

Daemo. Is this the one?

Palaes. That's it! O my beloved parents,
Here enclosed I keep you both;
Here I've stored my wealth, my hopes
Of ever recognizing you.   1145

Gripus Then, by Herc, whoever you are,
The gods must be enraged at you
For squeezing your beloved parents
Into such a narrow space.

Daemo. Here, Gripus! It's your day in court.
(*to* PALAESTRA) Young lady, move away a little;
State the contents, then describe them,
Listing each and every one.
If you make one minute mistake,
And later on insist that you   1150
Should be allowed a second chance—
In that case, lady, save your breath!

Gripus Very good! That's just!

Trach.   Then not like you:
You're very bad and unjust, too.

Daemo. Go ahead and speak, my girl.
Gripus, shape up and pipe down!

Palaes. There are some trinkets.

Daemo.   I see those.

Gripus (*aside*) A knockout in the opening round!
(*to* DAEMONES) Hang on, don't show them to her!

Daemo.   What do they
Look like? Answer one by one.   1155

Palaes. First, an itty-bitty sword
Of gold, inscribed with letters.

Daemo.   Tell me,
What are the letters on this itty-
Bitty sword?

Palaes.   My father's name.
Right beside it you will find
A teeny-weeny double axe,
Likewise gold, with letters; there
My mother's name appears.

Daemo.   Hold on!
What is your father's name on the little
Sword? Just say it!

Palaes.   Daemones.   1160

Daemo.   Ye gods eternal, where are all
My hopes?

Gripus   Sweet Pollux, where are mine?

Trach.   Continue, please! Immediately!

Gripus   Calm down, or go and hang yourselves!

Daemo.   Tell us your mother's name that's here
Upon the teeny-weeny axe.

Palaes.   Daedalis.

Daemo.   The gods are calling
Me to heaven!

Gripus   And me to hell!

Daemo.   This has to be my daughter, Gripus.

Gripus   Let her be, for all I care.   1165
(*to* TRACHALIO) May all the gods demolish you
For setting eyes on me today,
And punish me, for lacking the sense

	To look around a hundred times Before I raised my fishing net, In case someone was watching me.	
Palaes.	Then there's a tiny silver sickle, Two little hands with fingers clasped, A wee, small piglet—	
Gripus	Go to blazes With your precious piggy-wig!	1170

Palaes.   There is a golden locket, too,
A birthday present from my father.

Daemo.   Here it is, indeed! I can't
Restrain myself from hugging you.
My daughter, bless you! I am he—
The father who reared you as a child.
I am Daemones; your mother,
Daedalis, is in the house.

Palaes.   Bless you, dear unhoped-for father!

Daemo.   How I delight in your embrace!   1175

Trach.   It warms my heart to see you reap
The fruits of love and loyalty.

Daemo.   Come on, Trachalio; if you're able,
Bring this trunk inside the house.

Trach.   Just look at poor old Gripus! Since
Affairs have not gone well for you,
Congratulations, Gripus!

Daemo.   Daughter,
Come, let's go and see your mother.
She'll be better able to
Pursue this question of the proofs: 1180
She handled you much more than I
And knows your tokens thoroughly.

Palaes. Let us all go in the house,
Since all our efforts have been shared.
Follow me, Ampelisca.

Ampel.   Heaven's
Kindness fills me with delight.

(FATHER *and* DAUGHTER *enter the cottage, along with* TRACHALIO
and AMPELISCA. GRIPUS *picks up his net and rope.*)

Gripus Well, I'm a numbskull, don't you think,
To catch that dreadful trunk today?
And when I'd caught it, not to hide it
Somewhere, safely stashed away?   1185
I thought it might prove stormy profit
When I saw it first appear,
Because it landed on my lap
In such a stormy atmosphere.
Great Herc! I'm sure that trunk contains
Great hoards of gold and silver pelf;
My wisest course of action is
To sneak inside and hang myself—

For just a little while, let's say,
Until my headache goes away.   1190
            (*exit into house*)

Act IV, Scene 5

Enter DAEMONES *from the cottage.*

Daemo. Eternal gods! Am I not fortunate
To find my daughter unexpectedly?
If gods have blessings to bestow on us,
They somehow answer decent people's prayers.
Today I had no hope, no confidence,   1195
Yet found my daughter unexpectedly.
I'll marry her to a fine, well-bred young man:
My kinsman, a freeborn Athenian.
I want him brought to me with all dispatch.
I told his slave to come out here, then head   1200

To the forum; I'm surprised he hasn't left.
I think I'll check the door. What's this I see?
My wife with her arms around our daughter's neck.
Her show of love is getting on my nerves!

Act IV, Scene 6

Daemo.   (*addressing* DAEDALIS *through the open door*)
Sometimes, my dear, it's preferable
To postpone kissing for a while.   1205
Get ready for me: I'll perform
The ritual, when I come in,
In honor of the household gods
Who have increased our family.
We've lambs and sacrificial pigs.
You women, why do you insist
On holding up Trachalio?
Ah, excellent! He's coming out.

(*Enter* TRACHALIO, *still speaking to the women inside.*)

Trach.   Wherever he is, I'll track him down
And bring my master Plesidippus   1210
Back to you at once.

Daemo.   Tell him
All the news about my daughter;
Ask him to abandon other
Business and come here.

Trach.   O.K.

Daemo.   Inform him I'll be giving him
My daughter as his wife.

Trach.   O.K.

Daemo.   I know his father, tell him; he's
A relative of mine.

Trach.   O.K.

Daemo.   Be quick!

Trach.   O.K.

Daemo.   Make sure he's here
For dinner to be served.

Trach.   O.K.   1215

Daemo.   (*exasperated*) "O.K." to everything?

Trach.   O.K.
But do you know what I want of you?
Remember what you promised me:
To get me free today.

Daemo.   (*mocking* TRACHALIO) O.K.

Trach.   Be sure to plead with Plesidippus
For my liberty.

Daemo.   O.K.

Trach.   And have your daughter plead as well;
She'll easily prevail.

Daemo.   O.K.

Trach.   And Ampelisca must become
My wife, when I am free.

Daemo.   O.K.   1220

Trach.   And my good service must bring in
Some tangible reward.

Daemo.   O.K.

Trach.   "O.K." to everything?

Daemo.   O.K.

I'm just repaying you in kind.
But hurry into town right now
And come back here again.

Trach.   O.K.
I'll soon be here. And meanwhile, you
Look after all the rest.

Daemo.   O.K.

(*As* TRACHALIO *disappears toward the town, stage right,* DAEMONES
addresses the audience.)

May Hercules K.O. the guy
For his impertinent O.K.'ing!   1225
My ears got plugged when he'd reply
"O.K.," whatever I was saying.

Act IV, Scene 7

As DAEMONES *moves to enter his house, he is intercepted by the emerging figure of*
GRIPUS.

Gripus   O.K. if I have a word with you, Daemones?

Daemo.   What's the trouble, Gripus?

Gripus   About that trunk:
Be sensible and keep a gift from heaven.

Daemo.   Does it seem fair to you that I should claim   1230
As mine another person's property?

Gripus   A thing that I found in the sea?

Daemo.   So much the better for the loser, then;
That doesn't make it any more your trunk.

Gripus   That's why you're poor: you're far too virtuous.

Daemo.   Gripus, Gripus, there are many snares   1235
          In life, where men get trapped by treachery.
          And usually they're loaded up with bait:
          If someone greedy nibbles at this bait,
          He's trapped within the snare by his own greed.
          The wise and clever man, who takes precautions,   1240
          Long enjoys the fruits of honesty.
          Your catch, I think, is likely to get caught,
          Departing with its dowry much increased.
          Should I conceal an object I've been brought,
          Knowing it belongs to someone else?
          That's not at all like our friend Daemones!   1245
          Prudent masters always should avoid
          Conspiring in misconduct with their slaves.
          Profit by collusion's not for me!

Gripus   In theaters I've watched comedians
           Make sage remarks like yours, and win applause   1250
           By mouthing moral maxims to the crowd;
           But each of the audience, as he headed homeward,
           Failed to live the way that he'd been told.

Daemo.   Go in; don't bother me; control your tongue!
           I won't give you a thing, make no mistake!   1255

Gripus   Whatever's in that trunk, be it silver or gold,
           I pray it all may turn to ashes now!
                              (*exit into house*)

Daemo.   That's why we have such worthless slaves.
           For if he had joined forces with some slave,
           He'd have implicated both of them in theft;   1260
           He'd think he had a catch, but meanwhile he'd
           Be caught himself, and catch would lead to capture.
           Now I'll go in and sacrifice, and then
           I'll order dinner cooked for us at once.
                              (*exit into house*)

Act IV, Scene 8

From the city, stage right, enter PLESIDIPPUS *and* TRACHALIO, *in excellent spirits.*

Plesid.	Tell me your tale a second time,	
	My soul mate, my Trachalio,	1265
	My freedman; no, my patron, rather!	
	I might even say, my father.	
	Has Palaestra really found	
	Her father and mother?	

Trach. Found them both.

Plesid. She comes from Athens?

Trach. I believe.

Plesid. She's going to marry me?

Trach. I suspect.

Plesid. Will we become engaged today,
Do you imagine?

Trach. I imagine.

Plesid. Should I congratulate her father
Because he found her?

Trach. I imagine. 1270

Plesid. What of her mother?

Trach. I imagine . . .

Plesid. What?

Trach. Whatever you imagine.

Plesid. Can you imagine just how much
She matters to me?

Trach. I imagine.

Plesid. *I'm* right here; must *you* be so
Imaginary?

Trach. I imagine.

Plesid. Should I go running?

Trach.	I imagine.
Plesid.	Or walk demurely? (*demonstrating*)
Trach.	I imagine.
Plesid.	On my arrival, should I greet her?
Trach.	I imagine.
Plesid.	Then her father?

1275

Trach.	I imagine.
Plesid.	And her mother?
Trach.	I imagine.
Plesid.	Then what happens? Should I also throw my arms Around her dad?
Trach.	I don't imagine.
Plesid.	Give mom a hug?
Trach.	I don't imagine.
Plesid.	Kiss my girl?
Trach.	I don't imagine.
Plesid.	Damn! You've no imagination When I'm counting on you most.[20]
Trach.	You're off your rocker. Follow me!
Plesid.	Lead on, dear patron, where thou wilt!

1280

(*They enter Daemones' house.*)

---

[20]In this scene, Trachalio's repeated answer (*censeo*) admits a remarkable variety of meanings: "I think so," "I value," "I assess" (as a Roman censor), and "I express my formal opinion" (as a Roman senator). In using an English verb that is only roughly parallel, I have slightly changed the meaning of several lines.

ACT V

Enter the thoroughly dejected LABRAX *from the forum, stage right.*

Act V, Scene 1

Labrax   Is any other man alive
Today more miserable than me?
I was condemned by Plesidippus
To the Board of Restitution,
By whose verdict now Palaestra's
Taken from me. I'm destroyed!
I really think that pimps must be
The children of the goddess Fun,
Since everybody finds it funny
When disaster strikes a pimp.   1285
I'll now check out my other girl
Who's inside Venus' temple here;
I must at least abscond with this
Last remnant of my tattered life.

Act V, Scene 2

Enter GRIPUS *from Daemones' cottage. He is carrying a rusty spit, which he has been assigned to polish. In a disgruntled soliloquy, he addresses the absent members of his household.*

Gripus   I swear to Pollux, by tonight
No Gripus will you see alive
Unless the trunk's returned to me.

Labrax   (*aside*) I almost die whenever I hear
Anyone mention the word "trunk":
It bumps my breast like a battering ram.   1290

Gripus   That criminal's a free man now;

303

But I, the man who found the trunk
And caught it in my net at sea,
Get nothing out of you at all.

Labrax   (*aside*) Eternal gods! This fellow has
Pricked up my ears with his remarks.

Gripus   I'll post announcements everywhere,
By Herc, in letters two feet high:
"If anyone has lost a trunk
Containing heaps of gold and silver,   1295
Come see Gripus." You folks all
Expect to keep it, but you won't!

Labrax   (*aside*) Holy Herc! This fellow knows
Who has my trunk, I do believe.
I really must approach the man.
Ye gods, please lend me your support.

Gripus   (*mistaking the source of Labrax's voice*)
Why do you call me in? I want
To do my cleaning out of doors.
Sweet Pollux, this thing is composed
Of solid rust and not of iron: 1300
The more I try to polish it,
The redder and thinner it becomes.
It must be an enchanted spit,
The way it's aging in my hands.

Labrax   Good day, young man.

Gripus   And God bless you,
Old shaggy mop.

Labrax   What's up with you?

Gripus   All spit and polish.

Labrax   You keeping well?

Gripus   Why ask? Are you some kind of curer?

Labrax   Hardly! Add one syllable.   1305

Gripus	Procurer, then?

Labrax　　　　　　　You've hit the nail
Upon the head.[21]

Gripus　　　　　　　You look the part.
But what's your problem?

Labrax　　　　　　　　Just last night
Another man and I were shipwrecked.
There and then I lost (how dreadful!)
Everything that I possessed.

Gripus　What did you lose?

Labrax　　　　　　　I lost a trunk
Along with heaps of gold and silver.

Gripus　Do you remember the actual contents
Of that trunk that went astray?　　　　　　　　　　1310

Labrax　What does it matter? It's gone.

Gripus　　　　　　　　　　And yet—

Labrax　Enough! Let's talk of something else.

Gripus　What if I know who found your trunk?
I want to learn the particulars.

Labrax　It held eight hundred golden pieces,
Packed inside a money pouch;
A hundred minas' worth of Philips[22]
In a separate leather bag.

Gripus　(*aside*) Great Herc! What a tremendous haul!
I'll get a generous reward.　　　　　　　　　　1315

---

[21] I have adapted a Plautine exchange that runs as follows: "L. You keeping well? G. Why ask? You're not a *medicus* (doctor), are you? L. No! I'm one letter more than a *medicus*. G. Then you're a *mendicus* (beggar)? L. You've hit the nail, etc.

[22] Philip of Macedon minted famous golden coins in the fourth century B.C., not long before Diphilus wrote the original Greek play; there were five Philips to a mina. The scene that follows can be understood without any knowledge of Hellenistic Greek currency. The value of a didrachm (pronounced "*die*-dram") may be gauged by Ampelisca's purchase price of a thousand didrachms (equivalent to twenty minas), a standard price for a Plautine slave girl. A talent is a very large sum of money: sixty minas or three thousand didrachms.

The gods take heed of human need;
I'll go away with loads of loot.
It's obviously this man's trunk.
(*aloud*) Continue! Other details, please.

Labrax   A silver talent (proper measure)
Will be found inside a purse,
Besides a mixing bowl, a goblet,
Ladle, jug, and water pot.

Gripus   My goodness! Certainly you had
A glittering array of wealth.   1320

Labrax   That "had" is such a wretched word
When one has absolutely nil.

Gripus   What would you give a man who could
Disclose your goods and track them down?
A quick and ready answer, please!

Labrax   Three hundred didrachms.

Gripus   Balderdash!

Labrax   Four hundred.

Gripus   Stinky little scraps!

Labrax   Five hundred.

Gripus   Empty peanut shells!

Labrax   Six hundred.

Gripus   Now you're talking
Teeny-weeny little weevils!   1325

Labrax   How about seven hundred, then?

Gripus   You're puffing hot air; cool your mouth.

Labrax   I'll give a thousand didrachms.

Gripus   Dreamer!

Labrax	That's my limit.
Gripus	Take off!
Labrax	Listen: If I leave, your hopes are gone. Eleven hundred?
Gripus	You're asleep!
Labrax	Then state the amount you would demand.
Gripus	A sum you needn't supplement: A talent—three grand on the nose; And not a didrachm less will do. So just say either yes or no.
Labrax	(*aside*) What's to be done? I have no choice. (*aloud*) I'll pay the talent.
Gripus	(*moving toward the altar*) Step this way. I want our Venus to question you.
Labrax	Command me as you will.
Gripus	Then touch This altar of Venus.
Labrax	I'm touching it.
Gripus	You've got to swear an oath by Venus.
Labrax	What do I swear?
Gripus	What I declare.
Labrax	Then dictate anything you like. (*aside*) I don't need help inventing oaths.
Gripus	Then grasp the altar here.
Labrax	I've got it.

1330

1335

Gripus	Swear that you will pay me money On the selfsame day that you Retrieve that trunk of yours.

Labrax	Agreed.
	(*with formal religious solemnity*) Venus of Cyrene, so I swear: If I track down that trunk I lost at sea And if it's then restored to my possession With its gold and silver safe inside, Then to this person—	1340

Gripus	"Then to this person *Gripus*," say, and touch me.

Labrax	Then to this person Gripus (honest to Venus!) I'll give a silver talent right away.

Gripus	And if you cheat me, beg that Venus will Obliterate you in your line of trade. (*aside*) I hope this happens to you anyhow!	1345

Labrax	Dear Venus, if I fail to keep this oath, Give every pimp a life of misery.

Gripus	That's probable, however you behave. Wait here. I'll ask the old man to come out. Demand that trunk from him without delay. (*exit into house*)	1350

Labrax	Even if he does return that trunk, He won't be getting a penny out of me. It's my decision what my tongue should swear. But I'll shut up; he's back with the old man.	1355

Act V, Scene 3

GRIPUS *returns with* DAEMONES, *who is carrying the trunk.*

Gripus	This way.

Daemo.	Where's that pimp?

Gripus	Hey you,
	Look here! This gentleman has your trunk.

Daemo. I have it, I admit I do,
And you may have it if it's yours.
The contents, just as they were, will all
Be safely handed back to you.
Take it, if it's yours.

Labrax   Eternal
Gods! It's mine. Dear trunk, hello!   1360

Daemo. It's yours?

Labrax   You're asking me? By Herc,
Though Jove possessed it, it's still mine.

Daemo. Everything inside is safe;
One little box has been removed,
Along with trinkets by whose help
I got my daughter back today.

Labrax Who's she?

Daemo.   Palaestra, who was yours,
Has been discovered as my girl.

Labrax Holy Herc, congratulations!
I'm delighted things turned out   1365
So nicely, to your satisfaction.

Daemo. Thank you, but I don't buy that.

Labrax Yes, really! And as evidence
Of my delight, don't pay me (please!)
A penny for her; you're excused.

Daemo. Dear Pollux, you are generous!

Labrax Not so; it's actually you.

Gripus See here, you! Now you have the trunk.

Labrax	I have.
Gripus	Then hurry.
Labrax	To do what?
Gripus	To give me the money that you owe. 1370
Labrax	I swear to Pollux, I have neither Gift nor debt for you.
Gripus	What game Is this? No debt?
Labrax	No, none at all.
Gripus	Didn't you swear an oath to me?
Labrax	I swore an oath; I'll swear one now On any subject that I like: Oaths were invented for preserving, Not for losing property.
Gripus	Just hand me over a talent weight Of silver, you great perjurer! 1375
Daemo.	Gripus, what talent are you now Demanding of him?
Gripus	One he swore He'd give me.
Labrax	I just like to swear. (*to* DAEMONES) Are you some priest of perjury?
Daemo.	For what consideration did he Pledge you money?
Gripus	If I could Restore this trunk to his possession, Then he swore he would present me With a silver talent.

Labrax	(*to* GRIPUS) Find
	Somebody I can take to court; 1380
	I'll prove you acted under false
	Pretenses, and that I've not reached
	The legal age of twenty-five.[23]
Gripus	(*indicating* DAEMONES) Deal with him.
Labrax	No, someone else.
	I'll never carry off my trunk
	If I get him condemned in court.
Daemo.	And did you promise him the money?
Labrax	Yes, I admit it.
Daemo.	What you promised
	To my slave reverts to me.
	Don't be supposing, pimp, that you 1385
	Can use your pimpish standards here:
	No way!
Gripus	(*to* LABRAX) Did you believe you'd found
	A victim you could cheat at will?
	(*extending his hand*) Cold cash must be delivered here;
	I'll hand it over on the spot
	To this man, who will set me free.
Daemo.	(*to* LABRAX) Because I've acted graciously,
	Preserving all these articles
	For you, through my good offices—
Gripus	Oh, no, through mine! Please don't say yours. 1390
Daemo.	(*to* GRIPUS) Act sensibly; shut up! (*to* LABRAX)—You should
	Be gracious to me in return,
	Obliging me as I deserve.

---

[23] A Roman law (the *Lex Plaetoria*) prevented a minor under the age of twenty-five from entering into a binding contract (see *Pseudolus,* line 303). Of course, Labrax's claim to be underage is nonsense. As a slave, Gripus cannot appear in court himself. Labrax does not want Daemones to be Gripus' representative, because he is afraid of alienating him and risking the loss of his trunk.

Labrax	I gather your request concedes
	My right of ownership?
Daemo.	It's quite
	Astonishing I haven't risked
	Aspiring to that right of yours!
Gripus	(*aside*) I'm safe: the pimp is wavering;
	My freedom's indicated now.
Daemo.	This fellow found your precious trunk,
	And he is legally my slave.
	What's more, I kept it safe for you,
	With all the money it contained.
Labrax	I'm grateful. As far as the talent goes,
	I see no reason why you shouldn't
	Get what I promised him.
Gripus	All right!
	You'd better give it to me, then.
Daemo.	Be quiet!
Gripus	You pretend to serve
	My cause, then feather your own nest.
	I may have lost the other prize,
	But you won't swindle me of this!
Daemo.	You'll get a flogging if you add
	One single word.
Gripus	Then kill me off!
	The only way to silence me's
	To stuff a talent in my mouth!
Labrax	He has your interests at heart.
	Shut up!
Daemo.	Step this way, pimp.
Labrax	All right.

1395

1400

(DAEMONES *and* LABRAX *move away from* GRIPUS, *in order to have a private conversation.*)

Gripus   Keep things up front; I never like
Low mumbling or whispering.

Daemo.   (*sotto voce*) Tell me, what was the price you paid
To buy your other little lady,   1405
Ampelisca?

Labrax   I shelled out
A thousand didrachms.

Daemo.   Would you like
To hear a dazzling proposition?

Labrax   Yes, I'd like that very much.

Daemo.   I'll split the talent up two ways.

Labrax   That sounds good.

Daemo.   For the second girl,
To buy her freedom you take half,
Then give the other half to him.

Labrax   By all means.

Daemo.   In return for that half,
I'll make Gripus a free man,
Acknowledging his role in finding
You a trunk and me a daughter.   1410

Labrax   Well done! I am most obliged.

Gripus   (*who has not heard any of this conversation*)
How soon do I receive the cash?

Daemo.   The money's paid. I have it here.

Gripus   By Herc! I'd rather have it here.

Daemo.   (*teasing* GRIPUS)
By Herc! There's none for you, so don't
Suppose there is. I want you to
Release him from his oath.

Gripus   I'm through!
Unless I hang myself, I'm dead!   1415
I swear to Herc, from this time on
You'll never swindle me again.

Daemo.   Have dinner here tonight, dear pimp.

Labrax   That proposition's fine with me.

Daemo.   Both of you, follow me inside.
(*He moves downstage to address the audience.*)

Dear audience, I'd invite you all
   To dinner following the show,
Except there's nothing doing, and
   My groceries are running low;
And I imagine anyhow
   You must have somewhere else to go.   1420

But if you're willing to award
   A loud ovation to our play,
Come back and celebrate with me—
   In sixteen years from today.
(*looking directly at* GRIPUS)
You *both* will dine with me tonight.[24]

Gripus   All right!

Daemo.   Then clap your hands, this way.

(*exeunt omnes*)

---

[24]It would be strange and unsatisfying for the play to end with Gripus still ignorant of his impending freedom. Thus it may be assumed that Daemones' dinner invitation is given and received as a formal promise of manumission, since Roman slaves did not dine at table with their masters.